GoodFood magazine
101 LOW-FAT FEASTS

Published by BBC Worldwide Limited
Woodlands
80 Wood Lane
London W12 0TT

First published 2003
Reprinted in 2003 (twice), 2004 (five times), 2005 (six times), 2006
Copyright © BBC Worldwide 2003
All photographs © *BBC Good Food Magazine* 2003 and
BBC Vegetarian Good Food Magazine 2003

All the recipes contained in this book first appeared in *BBC Good
Food Magazine* and *BBC Vegetarian Good Food Magazine*.

ISBN 0 563 48840 9

Edited by Gilly Cubitt

Commissioning Editor: Vivien Bowler
Project Editors: Catherine Johnson and Sarah Miles
Designers: Kathryn Gammon and Annette Peppis
Design Manager: Sarah Ponder
Production Controller: Christopher Tinker

Set in Helvetica and ITC Officina Sans
Printed and bound in Italy by LEGO SpA
Colour origination by Radstock Reproductions Ltd, Midsomer Norton

GoodFood magazine

101 LOW-FAT FEASTS
TRIED-AND-TESTED RECIPES

Editor-in-chief
Orlando Murrin

Contents

Introduction   6

Introduction

Yes, it's possible! Low-fat recipes that don't cut corners on flavour or satisfaction. And this is no one-dish wonder – you'll find over 100 *BBC Good Food Magazine* recipes in this book to help keep you trim.

We've revamped everyday dishes, so you don't need to cut out your favourite meals, and we've introduced new and exciting recipes, like the *Chicken Skewers with Cucumber Dip* pictured opposite (see page 104 for recipe), to expand your repertoire. After all, when you're trying to eat less, it's important to make what you do have as delicious and tempting as possible.

Each recipe comes with a nutritional breakdown, so you can check not only calories and fat content, but also the

amount of saturated and unsaturated fats, which is crucial for those watching their cholesterol levels.

Our recipes have all been tried and tested in the Good Food kitchen, so we can guarantee fabulous results every time. This is lean cuisine with loads of flavours, no-fuss preparation and certainly no guilt. Use these recipes regularly and you will soon see the results you've been waiting for.

Orlando Murrin

Editor, *BBC Good Food Magazine*

Conversion tables

NOTES ON THE RECIPES
- Eggs are medium in the UK and Australia (large in America) unless stated otherwise.
- Wash all fresh produce before preparation.

OVEN TEMPERATURES

Gas	°C	Fan °C	°F	Oven temp.
¼	110	90	225	Very cool
½	120	100	250	Very cool
1	140	120	275	Cool or slow
2	150	130	300	Cool or slow
3	160	140	325	Warm
4	180	160	350	Moderate
5	190	170	375	Moderately hot
6	200	180	400	Fairly hot
7	220	200	425	Hot
8	230	210	450	Very hot
9	240	220	475	Very hot

APPROXIMATE WEIGHT CONVERSIONS
- All the recipes in this book list both imperial and metric measurements. Conversions are approximate and have been rounded up or down. Follow one set of measurements only; do not mix the two.
- Cup measurements, which are used by cooks in Australia and America, have not been listed here as they vary from ingredient to ingredient. Please use kitchen scales to measure dry/solid ingredients.

SPOON MEASURES

- Spoon measurements are level unless otherwise specified.
- 1 teaspoon = 5ml
- 1 tablespoon = 15ml
- 1 Australian tablespoon = 20ml (cooks in Australia should measure 3 teaspoons where 1 tablespoon is specified in a recipe)

APPROXIMATE LIQUID CONVERSIONS

metric	imperial	AUS	US
50ml	2fl oz	¼ cup	¼ cup
125ml	4fl oz	½ cup	½ cup
175ml	6fl oz	¾ cup	¾ cup
225ml	8fl oz	1 cup	1 cup
300ml	10fl oz/½ pint	½ pint	1¼ cups
450ml	16fl oz	2 cups	2 cups/1 pint
600ml	20fl oz/1 pint	1 pint	2½ cups
1 litre	35fl oz/1¾ pints	1¾ pints	1 quart

Try this soup, cooked only to the end of step one,
as a sauce for freshly cooked pasta too.

Roasted Tomato Soup

1 large onion, chopped
2 tbsp olive oil
1–2 garlic cloves
900g/2lb tomatoes, chopped
1 red pepper, seeded and chopped
4 carrots, chopped
600ml/1 pint vegetable stock
crusty bread, to serve

Takes 50 minutes • Serves 4

1 Preheat the oven to 200°C/Gas 6/fan oven 180°C. Toss together the onion, oil, garlic, tomatoes, pepper and carrots in a large roasting tin. Season with plenty of salt and freshly ground black pepper and roast for 40 minutes.

2 Pour over the stock and stir, scraping the bottom of the pan to release the scorched vegetable juices.

3 Transfer to a food processor and process until smooth. Transfer to a pan and gently reheat. Adjust the seasoning to taste and serve with toasted crusty bread.

• Per serving 155 kcalories, protein 4g, carbohydrate 21g, fat 7g, saturated fat 1g, fibre 6g, added sugar none, salt 0.61g

Use a soft-leafed English lettuce, for the best colour.
Time step two carefully or the green freshness will be lost.

Lettuce Soup

25g/1oz butter
1 onion, chopped
2 medium potatoes,
peeled and chopped
1 garlic clove
450ml/16fl oz vegetable stock
2 fresh lettuces, finely sliced
225ml/8fl oz milk
a little nutmeg
double cream and snipped chives,
to serve

Takes 40 minutes • Serves 8

1 Melt the butter in a large casserole with a lid, then stir in the onion, potato and garlic. Add the stock, season and simmer for 20 minutes, covered, until the potato is tender.
2 Add the lettuce and cook, covered, for 3–4 minutes until the stock returns to the boil and the lettuces are semi-wilted.
3 Liquidise, then return to the pan with the milk. Season, add a pinch of nutmeg and serve with a swirl of cream and a sprinkling of chives.

• Per serving 71 kcalories, protein 2g, carbohydrate 7g, fat 4g, saturated fat 2g, fibro 1g, added sugar none, salt 0.3g

To make deep-fried sage leaves, drop clean dry leaves into deep hot oil for a few seconds until crisp, but still green.

Cream of Pumpkin Soup

1.3kg/3lb pumpkin, peeled, sliced and seeded
3 tbsp olive oil
1 large onion, chopped
2 garlic cloves, chopped
2 tsp cumin seeds
1 potato, peeled and chopped
6 fresh thyme sprigs or 1 tsp dried
700ml/1¼ pints vegetable stock
crème fraîche, to serve
deep-fried sage leaves, to garnish

Takes 45 minutes • Serves 6

1 Cut the pumpkin into chunks. Heat the oil in a large pan, then fry the onion, garlic and cumin for 2–3 minutes. Add the pumpkin and potato and fry, stirring for 5–6 minutes. Add the leaves from the thyme sprigs (or use dried) to the pan.
2 Pour in the stock and simmer for about 15 minutes until the pumpkin and potato are soft. Whizz in a blender until smooth, then pour into a pan, heat through and season.
3 Serve each portion with crème fraîche, lightly stirred in. Garnish with fried sage leaves.

• Per serving 122 kcalories, protein 2g, carbohydrate 11g, fat 8g, saturated fat 1g, fibre 2g, added sugar none, salt 0.4g

This is a mildly spiced soup perfect for chilly evenings.
Reheat leftovers for lunch next day.

Sweet Potato and Lentil Soup

100g/4oz red lentils
(no need to soak)
1 onion, chopped
knob of butter
1 garlic clove, finely chopped
2 tbsp curry paste
450g/1lb orange sweet potatoes,
peeled and cubed
450g/1lb floury potatoes,
peeled and cubed
1.2 litres/2 pints hot vegetable stock
2 tbsp chopped fresh mint (optional)
142ml carton natural yogurt
naan bread, to serve

Takes 40 minutes • Serves 4

1 Cook the lentils in boiling water for 15 minutes. Cook the onion in the butter for 8 minutes until softened and beginning to brown. Stir in the garlic, curry paste and cubed potatoes. Cook for 5 minutes, stirring.
2 Drain the lentils. Add to the potatoes with the stock and cook for 12–15 minutes until the potatoes are fully cooked. Whizz in a blender until smooth. Return to the pan, season to taste and heat through.
3 Stir the mint, if using, into the yogurt and season to taste. Ladle the soup into bowls and swirl in the yogurt. Serve with naan bread.

• Per serving 330 kcalories, protein 14g, carbohydrate 63g, fat 4g, saturated fat 1g, fibre 6g, added sugar none, salt 1.53kg

Choose the least knobbly artichokes
you can find to make peeling easier.

Jerusalem Artichoke Soup

25g/1oz butter
2 onions, sliced
800g/1lb 2oz Jerusalem artichokes
600ml/1 pint vegetable stock,
or water in which you
have boiled potatoes
pinch of sugar
600ml/1 pint milk
knob of butter or 2 tbsp cream,
to finish
croûtons, to serve

Takes 1¼ hours • Serves 8

1 Heat the butter in a large casserole. Add the onions, cover and let them sweat for 5 minutes until soft but not brown. Peel and slice the artichokes, add to the onions and sweat for 15 minutes or until just tender.
2 Pour in the stock or potato water, and season with salt, white pepper and the sugar. Simmer for 20 minutes until soft.
3 Liquidise in batches, then pour back into the pan along with the milk. Bring to the boil, then stir in the butter or cream. Serve with croûtons.

• Per serving 179 kcalories, protein 5g, carbohydrate 19g, fat 10g, saturated fat 6g, fibre 3g, added sugar trace, salt 0.61g

A glorious clear pink soup with matchstick vegetables.
Add a spoonful of soured cream to serve.

Chunky Beetroot Soup

2 large, raw beetroot, peeled
2 large carrots, peeled
2 celery sticks
2 garlic cloves
4 large tomatoes, skinned
50g/2oz butter
1 large onion, thinly sliced
1.7 litres/3 pints vegetable stock
sprig of parsley, 1 bay leaf and
2 whole cloves, tied in muslin
142ml carton soured cream,
to serve

Takes 2 hours • Serves 8

1 Cut the beetroot, carrots and celery into thick matchsticks. Crush the garlic and chop the tomatoes. Heat the butter in a large pan or flameproof casserole and add the onion, beetroot, carrots and celery.
2 Cook gently for 10 minutes over a low heat, stirring occasionally. Add the garlic and tomatoes and continue to cook for another 5 minutes. Pour in the stock, season well and add the herbs and spices tied in muslin. Cover and simmer for 1½ hours.
3 When the time is up, remove the muslin bag and check the soup for seasoning. Serve in bowls with a dollop of soured cream in each.

• Per serving 89 kcalories, protein 2g, carbohydrate 8g, fat 6g, saturated fat 3g, fibre 2g, added sugar none, salt 0.89g

A simple soup that allows the flavour of
fresh summer vegetables to shine through.

Vegetable and Pesto Soup

1 tbsp olive oil
1 onion, chopped
225g/8oz new potatoes, sliced
1 vegetable stock cube
100g/4oz runner beans, sliced
450g/1lb courgettes,
sliced then halved
2–3 tbsp pesto

Takes 30 minutes • Serves 4

1 Heat the oil in a large pan and fry the onion for 8 minutes until golden. Add the potato slices and mix well. Dissolve the stock cube in 1.2 litres/2 pints boiling water, then add to the pan. Bring to the boil then simmer for 7 minutes until the potatoes are just cooked.

2 Add the runner beans to the pan and continue to cook for 5 minutes, adding the courgettes for the last 2 minutes of cooking time.

3 Season with plenty of salt and pepper. Remove from the heat and stir in two table-spoons of the pesto. Taste and add more pesto if necessary. Serve hot.

• Per serving 159 kcalories, protein 5g, carbohydrate 14g, fat 10g, saturated fat 2g, fibre 3g, added sugar none, salt 1.54g

Vary the combination of vegetables to suit yourself; even a bag of prepared stir-fry vegetables from the supermarket would do.

Asian Vegetable Broth

1 stalk lemon grass, thinly sliced
2.5cm/1in piece fresh ginger, sliced
2 garlic cloves, sliced
4 tbsp soy sauce
2 tbsp saké or dry sherry
finely grated zest and juice of 1 lime
1 tsp caster sugar
2 tbsp vegetable oil
2 carrots, cut into matchsticks
100g/4oz baby corn, halved
1 large red chilli, sliced
100g/4oz oyster mushrooms, sliced
50g/2oz baby spinach leaves
85g/3oz beansprouts

Takes 20 minutes • Serves 4

1 Place the lemon grass, ginger and garlic in a large pan with the soy sauce, saké or sherry, lime zest and juice and caster sugar. Add 850ml/1½ pints water and bring to the boil. Cover and simmer for 10 minutes. Strain and keep the broth warm.

2 Heat the oil in a large frying pan or wok, add the carrots, corn and chilli and stir-fry for 2 minutes. Add the mushrooms, spinach and beansprouts and remove from the heat.

3 Divide the vegetables between four serving bowls, pour over the hot broth and serve immediately.

• Per serving 130 kcalories, protein 4g, carbohydrate 9g, fat 8g, saturated fat 1g, fibre 3g, added sugar 1g, salt 2.3g

Look for fresh Japanese udon or yakisoba
noodles in the ethnic section of the supermarket.

Meal-in-a-bowl Noodle Soup

1 tsp vegetable oil
4–5 mushrooms, sliced
1 garlic clove, finely chopped
½ red pepper, seeded and
cut into strips
small stalk of broccoli,
broken into florets
211g pack fresh soupy udon
or yakisoba noodles

Takes 15 minutes • Serves 1
(easily doubled)

1 Heat the oil in a medium pan. Add the mushrooms, garlic, red pepper and broccoli and stir fry until the vegetables are beginning to soften, about 4 minutes.
2 Add the noodles. Stir in the contents of the flavouring sachet from the noodle pack and pour over 300ml/½ pint boiling water.
3 Cook the noodles for 2 minutes until they are tender and piping hot.

• Per serving 457 kcalories, protein 16g, carbohydrate 84g, fat 9g, saturated fat 0.2g, fibre 5g, added sugar none, salt 0.02g

A meal-in-a-bowl soup, full of colour and flavour.
You can freeze it for up to 1 month.

Chunky Fish Chowder

1 large onion, thinly sliced
500g/1lb 2oz potaotes, peeled and
cut into small chunks
1.2 litres/2 pints milk
1 garlic clove, crushed
300g can sweetcorn
kernels, drained
450g/1lb skinless smoked haddock
2 tbsp chopped fresh parsley
crusty brown bread, to serve

Takes 30–40 minutes • Serves 4

1 Put the onion and potatoes into a large saucepan, pour the milk over and season well with freshly ground black pepper. Bring to the boil, cover and simmer for 10 minutes, stirring occasionally.
2 Stir in the garlic, sweetcorn and fish, bring back to the boil, cover and simmer for 5 minutes.
3 Flake the fish into bite-size pieces with a fork. Stir in the parsley and season to taste. Serve with crusty brown bread.

• Per serving 417 kcalories, protein 36g, carbohydrate 57g, fat 7g, saturated fat 3g, fibre 3g, added sugar 5g, salt 3.04g

A quick and easy no-cook soup made from supermarket ingredients. It makes an ideal packed lunch.

Tomato Salsa Soup

8 tomatoes (about 650g/1lb 7oz),
roughly chopped
½ medium or 1 small red onion,
roughly chopped
good handful of fresh coriander
500g carton passata
(Italian tomato sauce)
410g can cannellini beans, drained
handful of chopped fresh coriander
and tortilla chips, to serve

Takes 10 minutes • Serves 4

1 Put the tomatoes, onion and coriander in a food processor and pulse briefly to chop.
2 Tip into a large bowl with the passata and beans, then add 150ml/¼ pint water. Season and mix well.
3 Sprinkle with chopped coriander and serve with tortilla chips.

• Per serving 141 kcalories, protein 8g, carbohydrate 26g, fat 1g, saturated fat none, fibre 5g, added sugar 2g, salt 0.84g

Out of season, frozen peas work really well in this soup.
Serve with Italian-style crusty bread.

Chilled Fresh Pea Soup

25g/1oz butter
300g/10oz floury potatoes,
cut into cubes
bunch of spring onions, thinly sliced
850ml/1½ pints vegetable stock
900g/2lb peas in pods, podded,
or 225g/8oz fresh or frozen
podded peas
200g carton natural Greek yogurt
handful of fresh chives, snipped

Takes 30 minutes, plus chilling •
Serves 6

1 Melt the butter in a pan, then add the potatoes and stir well. Cover and cook gently for 5 minutes. Stir in the spring onions, then add the stock and bring to the boil.

2 Cover and cook for 10 minutes until the potatoes are just tender. Add the peas and cook for 3 minutes, then purée the soup in a food processor or blender.

3 Pour into a bowl and whisk in the yogurt, then leave to cool. When cool, cover with plastic film and chill until ready. Stir in the chives when ready to serve.

• Per serving 143 kcalories, protein 7g, carbohydrate 14g, fat 7g, saturated fat 4g, fibre 3g, added sugar none, salt 0.64g

To prepare asparagus snap off the woody bottom then boil, steam or roast. Parboiling then roasting only works for young asparagus.

Roast Asparagus with Garlic

350g/12oz asparagus
2 tbsp olive oil
1 large garlic clove,
cut into very thin slices
1 tbsp large capers in brine,
rinsed and drained
juice of ½ orange

Takes 20 minutes •
Serves 4 as a starter

1 Preheat the oven to 200°C/Gas 6/fan oven 180°C. Bring a large pan of water to the boil. Add the asparagus and boil for 2 minutes until crisp, but beginning to go tender.

2 Drain and refresh under cold water. Dry on kitchen paper. Pour the oil into a shallow roasting tin and roll the asparagus in it to coat.

3 Scatter over the garlic slivers and capers and roast for 8–10 minutes until the asparagus is tinged browned and cooked through – test by inserting a knife into a few spears. Sprinkle with orange juice, season with sea salt and serve warm.

• Per serving 79 kcalories, protein 3g, carbohydrate 3g, fat 6g, saturated fat 1g, fibre 2g, added sugar none, salt 0.06g

Parma ham fries to a crisp very quickly and the salty
flavour goes well with most green vegetables.

Beans with Crispy Ham

450g/1lb green beans, trimmed
1 tbsp olive oil
85g/3oz Parma ham or prosciutto,
torn into strips
1 bunch spring onions,
sliced diagonally
1 tbsp balsamic vinegar

Takes 20 minutes • Serves 6

1 Bring a pan of water to the boil, add
salt and blanch the beans for 3–4 minutes.
2 Meanwhile, heat the oil in a large frying
pan or wok and fry the ham until crispy.
Add the spring onions and the vinegar and
stir for 1 minute.
3 Drain the beans and tip them into the
pan. Toss to coat the beans in oil. Season
to taste and serve immediately.

• Per serving 68 kcalories, protein 6g, carbohydrate
3g, fat 4g, saturated fat 1g, fibre 2g, added sugar
none, salt 0.94g

Butternut squash has a lovely delicate flavour.
This recipe has a buttery taste without being high in fat.

Baked Buttery Squash

1 butternut squash, about
675g/1lb 8oz in weight
½ tsp paprika
3 tbsp snipped fresh chives
3 tbsp low-fat crème fraîche
1 thick slice of white bread,
crust removed, crumbled
into breadcrumbs
generous knob of butter, melted
25g/1oz grated parmesan

Takes 1 hour 10 minutes • Serves 2

1 Preheat the oven to 200°C/Gas 6/fan oven 180°C from cold. Halve the squash lengthways, then scoop out the seeds and fibres and discard. Season the squash well and put in a roasting tin half full of water. Cover with foil and bake for about 40 minutes until tender.

2 Drain, then transfer the squash to a board until cool enough to handle. Scrape the flesh into a bowl, leaving a thin border of flesh on the skin. Mix the paprika, chives and crème fraîche with the flesh and season.

3 Pile the mixture into the squash shells. Mix the breadcrumbs with the butter and parmesan and sprinkle on top. Bake for 15 minutes until lightly browned.

• Per serving 271 kcalories, protein 13g, carbohydrate 35g, fat 10g, saturated fat 6g, fibre 5g, added sugar none, salt 0.78g

Everyone loves jacket potato wedges and this saucy
version is especially popular with children.

Potato Wedges with Tuna

3 large baking potatoes
3 tbsp olive oil
1 leek, sliced
200g can tuna in brine, drained
2 × 400g cans chopped tomatoes
with chilli in tomato juice

Takes 35 minutes • Serves 4

1 Preheat the oven to 220°C/Gas 7/fan
oven 200°C. Cut the potatoes into wedges
and put in a roasting tin. Drizzle over two
tablespoons of the oil, making sure all the
potatoes are covered. Bake for 30 minutes
until crispy on the outside and soft inside.
2 Meanwhile, heat the remaining oil in
a pan and fry the leek until softened.
Tip in the tuna and the chilli tomatoes,
breaking the tuna down until well combined
with the tomatoes.
3 Cook for a few minutes until hot. Season
and spoon over the potatoes in the roasting
tin, mixing gently. Serve immediately.

• Per serving 264 kcalories, protein 16g, carbohydrate
32g, fat 9g, saturated fat 1g, fibre 5g, added sugar
none, salt 0.76g

Don't let the lengthy cooking time put you off.
The actual work takes only 10 minutes.

Jackets with Tuna and Chives

4 baking potatoes
250g tub 'virtually fat-free' cottage cheese with onions and chives
200g can good-quality tuna in water, drained
1 celery stick, sliced
3 spring onions, trimmed and sliced
Tabasco sauce and green salad, to serve

Takes 1½ hours • Serves 4

1 Preheat the oven to 180°C/Gas 4/fan oven 160°C. Prick the potatoes with a fork. Put them straight on to a shelf in the hottest part of the oven for 1–1¼ hours, or until they are soft inside.
2 Meanwhile, mix the cottage cheese with the tuna, celery, spring onions. Season.
3 To serve, cut a deep cross in each baked potato and spoon the filling on top. Sprinkle a few drops of Tabasco sauce over and serve with a green salad.

• Per serving 237 kcalories, protein 20g, carbohydrate 39g, fat 1g, saturated fat none, fibre 3g, added sugar none, salt 0.61g

A good-looking salad, and good for you too.
Horseradish is delicious with both trout and beetroot.

Trout, Beetroot and Bean Salad

225g/8oz fine green beans, trimmed
120g bag watercress and
rocket salad
2 tsp balsamic vinegar
250g pack cooked smoked
trout fillets
4 cooked beetroot, diced
6 tbsp 0% fat fromage frais
1–2 tbsp fresh lemon juice
2 tsp creamed horseradish

Takes 15 minutes • Serves 4

1 Cook the green beans in a pan of lightly salted boiling water for 3–4 minutes until just tender. Drain and refresh in cold water.
2 Put the salad leaves in a large bowl and season. Pour in the balsamic vinegar and toss well to coat. Arrange the dressed leaves on a serving dish. Flake the trout on to the leaves and top with the cooked beans and diced beetroot.
3 Mix the fromage frais, lemon juice and creamed horseradish and season to taste. Drizzle over the salad just before serving.

• Per serving 140 kcalories, protein 17g, carbohydrate 10g, fat 4g, saturated fat 1g, fibre 3g, added sugar none, salt 1.52g

An easy salad made from storecupboard ingredients,
perfect when you suddenly fancy a snack.

Tuna, Bean and Corn Salad

125g can tuna slices or 185g can
tuna chunks, drained
165g can sweetcorn
with peppers, drained
½ red onion, finely chopped
200g can red kidney beans, drained
2 handfuls mixed salad leaves
1 tbsp olive oil
2 tsp fresh lemon juice
pinch of mild chilli powder
toasted crusty bread, to serve

Takes 10 minutes • Serves 2
(easily doubled)

1 In a large bowl, mix the tuna lightly with the sweetcorn, onion and kidney beans. Season well.

2 Divide the salad leaves between two plates, season lightly, then pile the tuna salad on top.

3 Drizzle over the olive oil and lemon juice and sprinkle with the chilli. Serve with toasted crusty bread.

• Per serving 277 kcalories, protein 21g, carbohydrate 33g, fat 8g, saturated fat 1g, fibre 6g, added sugar 5g, salt 1.63g

A simple salad of crunchy vegetables in a warm dressing,
served with sticky sushi rice.

Japanese Salad with Rice

225g/8oz sushi rice
1 mooli (large white radish), peeled
2 carrots, peeled
1 small cucumber (about 250g/9oz)
3 tbsp mirin (Japanese sweet
rice wine) or dry sherry
2 tbsp rice wine vinegar
2 tbsp Japanese soy sauce
2 tsp caster sugar
coriander sprigs, to serve

Takes 20 minutes, plus standing •
Serves 4

1 Rinse the rice in a sieve in cold water until the water runs clear. Place in a pan and pour over 300ml/½ pint cold water, cover, then bring to the boil. Simmer for 10 minutes without removing the lid. Leave to stand, covered, for 10 minutes.

2 Meanwhile, cut the mooli, carrots and cucumber into matchsticks and place in a bowl. Put the remaining ingredients in a small pan and heat gently until steam starts to rise. Pour over the vegetables and marinate for 15 minutes.

3 Divide the rice between four serving plates, spoon the vegetables on top, then drizzle the dressing over. Serve immediately, topped with the coriander.

• Per serving 254 kcalories, protein 5g, carbohydrate 57g, fat 1g, saturated fat 0.03g, fibre 1g, added sugar 3g, salt 1.15g

This is a hearty salad, packed with
interesting textures and flavours.

Warm Potato and Spinach Salad

700g/1lb 9oz new potatoes,
scrubbed and halved
225g bag of baby spinach leaves
4 rashers of smoked back bacon,
trimmed of fat
175g/6oz button mushrooms,
thinly sliced
410g can butter beans, drained

FOR THE DRESSING
1 garlic clove, crushed
2 tsp wholegrain mustard
2 tsp balsamic vinegar
1 tbsp olive oil

Takes 30 minutes • Serves 4

1 Cook the potatoes in salted boiling water
for 8–10 minutes until just tender. Drain and
immediately toss with the spinach leaves
so they wilt very slightly. Set aside.

2 Grill the bacon for 5–6 minutes until the
rashers are very crisp. Drain on kitchen
paper. Mix all the dressing ingredients in
a large bowl. Add the mushrooms and
butter beans, season and leave to stand for
5 minutes.

3 Add the potatoes, spinach and bacon to
the mushrooms, then toss together. Serve
at once.

• Per serving 282 kcalories, protein 14g, carbohydrate
39g, fat 9g, saturated fat 2g, fibre 7g, added sugar
none, salt 1.94g

A healthy and colourful alternative
to eggs on toast.

Pepper and Egg Sauté

1 tbsp olive oil
1 large onion, finely chopped
2 garlic cloves, crushed
2 yellow peppers, seeded and
finely sliced
300g/10oz French beans,
cut into 5cm/2in pieces
8 tbsp white wine
4 ripe tomatoes, diced
4 medium eggs
4 tbsp chopped fresh flatleaf parsley
crusty bread, to serve

Takes 25 minutes • Serves 4

1 Heat the olive oil in a large frying pan and fry the onion and garlic for 2 minutes until softened. Add the yellow peppers, French beans and white wine. Fry, stirring for a further 2–3 minutes.

2 Add the diced tomatoes and cook for 1–2 minutes until warmed through. Make four hollows in the vegetable mixture with the back of a spoon.

3 Crack an egg into each one and cook over a medium heat for 3–4 minutes until the egg is set to your liking. Sprinkle over the parsley and season well. Serve with crusty bread.

• Per serving 187 kcalories, protein 10g, carbohydrate 11g, fat 10g, saturated fat 2g, fibre 4g, added sugar none, salt 0.23g

A no-cook lunch packed with vitamins. Eat straightaway,
while the pears and watercress are fresh and crisp.

Ham and Pear Open Sandwiches

3 tbsp thick honey
1 tbsp Dijon mustard
2 tsp soft dark brown sugar
4 thick slices of sourdough
rye bread
1 ripe but firm Conference or
William pear
4 slices Parma ham
large handful of watercress

Takes 10 minutes • Serves 2

1 Mix together the honey, mustard and
soft dark brown sugar to a smooth paste.
2 Spread the honey mixture over the
bread slices. Cut the pear in half lengthways
without peeling it, and core and discard the
pips. Cut it into thick slices.
3 Cover each piece of bread with slices of
pear and top with slices of Parma ham. Add
a pile of watercress leaves and grind pepper
over the top. Serve straightaway.

• Per serving 315 kcalories, protein 13g, carbohydrate
58g, fat 5g, saturated fat 1g, fibre 4g, added sugar
23g, salt 2.75g

Spicy chickpea cakes make a tasty filling
for a hot pitta bread sandwich.

Falafel Pittas

2 × 400g cans chickpeas, drained
1 small onion, roughly chopped
2 carrots, roughly chopped
1 large garlic clove,
roughly chopped
1 tsp ground coriander
1 tsp ground cumin
small handful of parsley sprigs
oil, for brushing
6 pitta breads
crispy lettuce, cucumber slices and
natural yogurt, to serve

Takes 25 minutes • Serves 6

1 Preheat the grill to medium. Put the chickpeas into a food processor with the onion, carrots, garlic, coriander, cumin, parsley, salt and pepper. Whizz briefly to retain some of the chunky texture in the chickpeas. Shape the mixture into six round cakes.

2 Carefully place the falafels on a grill pan lined with foil. Brush with a little oil. Grill for 4–5 minutes on each side. Meanwhile, toast the pitta breads and tear the lettuce into strips.

3 Stuff the hot falafels into the pitta breads. Add a small handful of torn lettuce, a few slices of cucumber and a drizzle of natural yogurt. Serve straightaway.

• Per serving 281 kcalories, protein 12g, carbohydrate 53g, fat 4g, saturated fat 0g, fibre 6g, added sugar none, salt 1.3g

This is a modern version of beans on toast.
Try it topped with stir-fried garlicky greens too.

Chicory, Bean and Chilli Crostini

2 tbsp olive oil
1 red onion, thinly sliced
2 garlic cloves, thinly sliced
1 red chilli, halved,
seeded and sliced
2 tbsp balsamic vinegar
420g can cannellini beans,
drained and rinsed
4 tbsp dry white wine
handful flatleaf parsley, roughly torn
4 thick slices crusty Italian bread
2 red chicory heads,
halved lengthways

Takes 20 minutes • Serves 4

1 Heat one tablespoon of the oil in a frying pan and fry the onion, garlic and chilli for 5 minutes until softened. Stir in the vinegar, beans and wine and cook for 3–4 minutes until all the liquid has evaporated. Stir in the parsley and season.
2 Meanwhile, brush the remaining oil over a griddle and heat until starting to smoke. Arrange the bread and chicory, cut-side down, on top and cook for 1 minute. Remove the chicory. Turn the bread over and brown the other side.
3 Divide the bread between serving plates and spoon the beans over. Place the chicory on top and season with freshly ground black pepper. Serve immediately.

• Per serving 302 kcalories, protein 11g, carbohydrate 38g, fat 12g, saturated fat 1g, fibre 8g, added sugar none, salt 1.15g

Unlike some Thai dishes these are not too hot,
just mildly spicy, perfect for a light supper or lunch.

Spicy Thai Fish Kebabs

1 tbsp Thai Lemon Grass and
Coconut Stir-Fry Seasoning
1 tsp vegetable oil
250g/9oz skinless plaice or pollack
fillets, cut into long strips
1 yellow pepper, seeded and
cut into chunks
1 onion, cut into chunks
4 cherry tomatoes
Thai jasmine rice, to serve

FOR THE DIP
1 tbsp chopped fresh parsley
150ml/¼ pint low-fat yogurt
lemon juice, to taste

Takes 20–30 minutes • Serves 2

1 Preheat the oven to 180°C/gas 4/fan
160°C. Line a baking tray with foil and brush
lightly with oil.
2 Mix the Thai seasoning and oil in a
shallow bowl and season well. Roll the fish
in the spice mixture, then loosely concertina
it on four skewers. Follow with two to three
chunks of pepper and onion per skewer
and finish with a cherry tomato.
3 Roast the skewers on the foil for
8–10 minutes or until the fish is white and
opaque. Stir the parsley into the yogurt,
then add the lemon juice and season to
taste. Serve with the kebabs and rice.

• Per serving 215 kcalories, protein 27g, carbohydrate
18g, fat 5g, saturated fat 1g, fibre 3g, added sugar
none, salt 2.07g

Take a few storecupboard basics and you can
have supper on the table in around 15 minutes.

Tomato and Olive Spaghetti

350g/12oz spaghetti
1 tbsp olive oil
2 garlic cloves, finely chopped
4 anchovy fillets in oil, drained
400g can plum tomatoes
100g/4oz pitted black olives,
roughly chopped
3 tbsp capers, rinsed and
roughly chopped
2 tbsp chopped fresh parsley

Takes 15 minutes • Serves 4

1 Stir the spaghetti into a large pan of salted
boiling water and cook for 12–15 minutes
until just tender.
2 Meanwhile, heat the oil in a pan and
cook the garlic and anchovies for 2 minutes.
Tip in the tomatoes and cook for 5 minutes,
breaking them lightly with a wooden spoon.
Stir in the olives and capers and cook for a
further 5 minutes. Season to taste and stir
in the parsley.
3 Drain the pasta well and return to the pan.
Stir in the sauce, divide between warmed
bowls and serve.

• Per serving 377 kcalories, protein 13g, carbohydrate
68g, fat 8g, saturated fat 1g, fibre 4g, added sugar
none, salt 1.98g

There's more to spaghetti than Bolognese.
Try this low-fat sauce made with a jar of cockles.

Seafood Spaghetti

175g/6oz spaghetti
1 tbsp olive oil
2 garlic cloves, finely chopped
400g can chopped tomatoes
200g jar of cockles in
vinegar, drained
pinch of dried chilli flakes
2 tbsp chopped fresh parsley

Takes 15 minutes • Serves 2
(easily doubled)

1 Cook the spaghetti in a pan of salted boiling water for 10–12 minutes until tender.
2 Meanwhile, heat the oil in a frying pan, then fry the garlic for 30 seconds. Add the tomatoes and bubble for 2–3 minutes. Add the cockles and chilli flakes, season, then stir to heat through.
3 Drain the spaghetti and return to the pan. Stir in the sauce and serve sprinkled with chopped parsley.

• Per serving 424 kcalories, protein 21g, carbohydrate 71g, fat 8g, saturated fat 1g, fibre 5g, added sugar none, salt 1.39g

The pasta sauce can be made up to two days in advance and chilled. Or thin it down with stock to make a tasty soup.

Pumpkin and Bean Spaghetti

2 tbsp olive oil
2 onions, thinly sliced
2 garlic cloves, crushed
350g/12oz diced pumpkin or butternut squash
400g can chopped tomatoes
400ml/14fl oz vegetable stock
350g/12oz spaghetti
420g can mixed beans in a mild chilli sauce
small handful finely grated parmesan, to serve

Takes 50 minutes • Serves 4

1 Heat the oil in a pan and fry the onions for 8 minutes, until softened. Add the garlic and pumpkin or squash and fry for a further 5 minutes. Stir in the tomatoes and stock. Bring to the boil, cover and simmer for 15 minutes, until the pumpkin is tender.
2 Meanwhile, cook the spaghetti in a large pan of salted boiling water according to the packet instructions.
3 Add the beans to the pasta sauce and cook for 3–4 minutes. Season to taste. Drain the spaghetti well, return to the pan, then stir in the sauce. Divide between shallow bowls and serve sprinkled with parmesan.

• Per serving 477 kcalories, protein 19g, carbohydrate 88g, fat 8g, saturated fat 1g, fibre 9g, added sugar none, salt 2.01g

If you love garlic, try adding a couple of
chopped cloves to the breadcrumbs.

Spaghetti with Broccoli and Anchovies

350g/12oz dried spaghetti
350g/12oz broccoli
5 tbsp olive oil
6 anchovies, chopped
2 fresh red chillies, seeded and
finely chopped
100g/4oz white breadcrumbs,
made with stale bread

Takes 25–30 minutes • Serves 4

1 Cook the spaghetti in a large pan of boiling water, according to the packet instructions. Cut the broccoli into small florets, thinly slice the thick stalks and throw into the pan of pasta for the last 3 minutes of cooking time.
2 Meanwhile, heat 3 tablespoons of olive oil in a frying pan, add the anchovies and chillies and fry briefly. Add the breadcrumbs and cook, stirring, for about 5 minutes until the crumbs are crunchy and golden.
3 Drain the spaghetti and return to the pan. Toss with three quarters of the crumb mixture, some salt and pepper and another 2 tablespoons of olive oil. Serve each portion sprinkled with the remaining crumbs.

• Per serving 400 kcalories, protein 17g, carbohydrate 78g, fat 4g, saturated fat 0.5g, fibre 5g, added sugar none, salt 0.8g

This simple recipe uses just five ingredients and
is excellent for using up tomatoes that are too soft for salad.

Creamy Tomato and Pepper Pasta

900g/2lb ripe tomatoes
1 red pepper
2 garlic cloves
350g/12oz pasta quills or shells
4 tbsp crème fraîche
grated parmesan, to serve

Takes 50 minutes • Serves 4

1 Preheat the oven to 200°C/Gas 6/fan oven 180°C. Quarter the tomatoes, roughly chop the pepper (discarding the seeds) and finely chop the garlic. Put them in a roasting tin and drizzle over three tablespoons of olive oil. Season well.

2 Roast for 30–35 minutes, stirring halfway through, until softened and slightly browned. Meanwhile, cook the pasta in a large pan of salted boiling water for 10–12 minutes until just tender (follow the packet instructions if you are using fresh pasta).

3 Remove the vegetables from the oven and stir in the crème fraîche a spoonful at a time. Bubble up on the stove to reheat, taste and season if necessary. Stir in the drained pasta and serve with grated parmesan.

• Per serving 419 kcalories, protein 13g, carbohydrate 77g, fat 9g, saturated fat 4g, fibre 6g, added sugar none, salt 0.38g

You can rustle up the ingredients for this tasty pasta
supper from cans and packets in the storecupboard.

Pasta with Tuna and Tomato

2 tbsp olive oil
1 onion, chopped
2 garlic cloves, finely chopped
400g can chopped tomatoes
with herbs
½ tsp chilli powder
1 tsp sugar
500g packet pasta bows
100g can tuna, drained
handful of basil leaves, optional

Takes 25 minutes • Serves 4

1 Heat the oil in a pan, add the onion
and cook for a couple of minutes. Stir in the
garlic, tomatoes, chilli and sugar. Season
and bring to the boil. Stir, then reduce the
heat and simmer for 5 minutes.
2 Meanwhile, bring a large pan of salted
water to the boil. Add the pasta and cook
according to packet instructions.
3 Flake the tuna into the sauce and heat
through. Drain the pasta, return to the pan
and stir in the sauce and basil leaves. Serve
with a generous grinding of pepper.

• Per serving 553 kcalories, protein 21g, carbohydrate
102g, fat 10g, saturated fat 1g, fibre 5g, added sugar
1g, salt 0.52g

This makes a great vegetarian family supper,
but it can easily be halved to serve two.

Summer Veggie Pasta

225g/8oz pasta bows
175g/6oz fresh or frozen broad
beans (about 650g/
1lb 7oz in their pods)
1 tbsp good-quality olive oil
1 large onion, finely chopped
2 garlic cloves, chopped
2 large courgettes, cut into sticks
6 ripe plum tomatoes,
cut into wedges
generous dash of Tabasco
handful of shredded basil

Takes 30 minutes • Serves 4

1 Cook the pasta according to the packet instructions, adding the fresh broad beans for the last 3 minutes (frozen ones for the last 2 minutes).
2 While the pasta is cooking, heat the oil in a large frying pan. Add the onion and cook over a medium heat for 1–2 minutes. Stir in the garlic and courgettes, toss over a medium heat for 2–3 minutes, then stir in the tomatoes and shake in the Tabasco. Stir for 2–3 minutes to soften the tomatoes a little (not too much or they will go mushy). Drain the pasta and beans.
3 Toss the vegetables and basil into the pasta and season. Serve hot (or cold as a salad with a low-fat dressing).

• Per serving 284 kcalories, protein 12g, carbohydrate 51g, fat 5g, saturated fat 1g, fibre 7g, added sugar none, salt 0.1g

Tangy goat's cheese goes wonderfully with the smoky peppers.
Try it with spaghetti or pasta shapes too.

Roast Tomato and Pepper Gnocchi

450g/1lb ripe tomatoes, halved
2 red peppers, cut into strips
2 garlic cloves, unpeeled
2 tbsp olive oil
500g pack fresh gnocchi
100g/4oz goat's cheese
fresh basil leaves and a green salad,
to serve

Takes 25 minutes • Serves 4

1 Preheat oven to 220°C/Gas 7/fan oven 200°C. Put the tomatoes, peppers and garlic and oil in a roasting tin. Sprinkle with salt and stir to coat. Roast for 20 minutes. Just before the tomatoes and peppers are done, cook the gnocchi in salted boiling water for 2–3 minutes or according to the packet instructions.

2 Remove the tomatoes, peppers and garlic from the oven. Squeeze the garlic from its skin and put in a food processor with the tomatoes, peppers and pan juices. Season. Whizz for a few seconds for a rough sauce.

3 Drain the gnocchi and transfer to a bowl. Pour the sauce over the gnocchi and mix gently. Divide between plates, crumble over the cheese and scatter over torn basil leaves. Serve with a green salad.

• Per serving 326 kcalories, protein 9g, carbohydrate 50g, fat 11g, saturated fat 1g, fibre 4g, added sugar none, salt 1.6g

Simple ingredients are given a flavour boost with fresh-tasting lemongrass, coriander and the fiery heat of chopped chilli.

Fragrant Rice with Chilli Vegetables

225g/8oz jasmine or Thai rice
1 stalk lemongrass, finely chopped
175g/6oz mangetout,
halved lengthways
175g/6oz baby sweetcorn,
halved lengthways
2 tomatoes, roughly chopped
25g/1oz fresh coriander,
finely chopped
25g/1oz desiccated coconut,
lightly toasted
1 red chilli, finely chopped
1 tbsp soy sauce
coriander sprigs, to serve

Takes 45 minutes • Serves 4

1 Half fill the base of a steamer with water. Bring to the boil and cover with the steamer layer and lid. Rinse the rice under cold running water. Drain and put into a basin (check it will fit into the steamer layer). Add the lemongrass, seasoning and 600ml/1 pint boiling water to the basin. Put into the steamer and put on the lid. Cook for 30 minutes until the rice has absorbed almost all the water.
2 Arrange the vegetables in the steamer, around the basin. Cover and steam for 2 minutes.
3 Stir the coriander, coconut and chilli into the rice and divide it between serving plates. Top with the vegetables and drizzle the soy sauce over. Serve topped with the coriander sprigs.

• Per serving 249 kcalories, protein 7g, carbohydrate 48g, fat 5g, saturated fat 3g, fibre 3g, added sugar none, salt 0.65g

This filling meal, ready in just 25 minutes, uses mostly storecupboard ingredients, keeping shopping to a minimum.

Tuna and Tomato Rice

225g/8oz long grain rice
1 tbsp olive oil
2 garlic cloves, finely chopped
1 onion, finely chopped
2 smoked streaky bacon rashers, chopped
175g/6oz chestnut mushrooms, sliced
2 × 400g cans chopped tomatoes
200g can tuna, drained
generous handful of fresh parsley, finely chopped
garlic bread, to serve

Takes 25 minutes • Serves 4

1 Cook the rice in salted boiling water for 10–12 minutes, or as directed on the packet.
2 Meanwhile, heat the oil in a pan and fry the garlic, onion and bacon for 5 minutes, stirring often. Add the mushrooms and cook for another 2–3 minutes. Stir in the tomatoes and tuna and season well. Heat through for 5 minutes.
3 Drain the rice, stir it into the tomato sauce with the parsley, mixing gently. Serve with garlic bread.

• Per serving 346 kcalories, protein 19g, carbohydrate 57g, fat 6g, saturated fat 2g, fibre 6g, added sugar 3g, salt 3.52g

Use your microwave to make perfect rice in next to
no time. You'll find risotto rice in most supermarkets.

Quick Fish Risotto

1 onion, finely chopped
1 garlic clove, finely chopped
1 vegetable or fish stock cube
250g/9oz risotto rice
250g/9oz smoked cod or haddock,
skinned and cut into chunks
large cupful of frozen peas
large knob of butter
1 lemon, cut into 8 wedges, to serve

Takes 20 minutes • Serves 4

1 Put the onion and garlic in a large
heatproof non-metallic bowl with the stock
cube and 300ml/½ pint boiling water. Stir
well, then cover and microwave on High for
3 minutes.
2 Stir in the rice with another 300ml/½ pint
boiling water, cover and microwave on High
for 10 minutes, stirring after 5 minutes.
3 Stir the fish into the rice with the peas
and another 300ml/½ pint boiling water.
Cover and microwave on High for 4 minutes.
Check the rice is cooked – if not, cook
for another minute. Leave to stand for
1–2 minutes for the liquid to be absorbed.
Stir in the butter and season well. Serve hot
with lemon wedges.

• Per serving 323 kcalories, protein 20g, carbohydrate
56g, fat 4g, saturated fat 2g, fibre 3g, added sugar
none, salt 3.1g

You'll find flat rice noodles with the oriental foods in the supermarket. Change the vegetables to suit your taste.

Zesty Noodle Stir Fry

140g/5oz flat rice noodles
6 tbsp soy sauce
5 tbsp fresh orange juice
½ tsp finely grated orange zest
1 tsp sugar
½ tsp cornflour
1 tbsp of vegetable or sunflower oil
½ tbsp grated fresh root ginger
2 garlic cloves, finely chopped
2 tbsp dry sherry
2 red peppers, seeded and sliced
2 carrots, peeled, cut into fine strips
2 courgettes cut into fine strips
100g/4oz mangetout, sliced
220g can water chestnuts, sliced
1 bunch spring onions, shredded

Takes 40 minutes • Serves 4
(easily halved)

1 Put the noodles in a large bowl, cover with boiling water for 4 minutes, then drain and rinse under cold water.
2 Mix the soy sauce, orange juice and zest, sugar and cornflour. Heat the oil in a wok, add the ginger and garlic and fry for 1 minute. Add the sherry and peppers and fry for 1 minute. Add the carrots, courgettes and mangetout and fry for 3 minutes. Stir in the water chestnuts and spring onions and fry for a minute.
3 Add the soy sauce mix and noodles and stir fry until hot. Serve straightaway.

• Per serving 240 kcalories, protein 6g, carbohydrate 47g, fat 3g, saturated fat 0g, fibre 4g, added sugar 1.6g, salt 2.77g

With a pack of egg noodles in your storecupboard
you have the basis of a versatile stir fry.

Chicken and Broccoli Noodles

250g packet egg noodles
350g/12oz broccoli florets
2 tbsp olive oil
2.5cm/1in piece fresh
root ginger, grated
4 garlic cloves, finely sliced
2 boneless skinless chicken breasts,
cut into thin strips
bunch of spring onions, trimmed
and cut in half horizontally, large
ones cut in half again vertically
3 tbsp soy sauce
200ml/7fl oz chicken or
vegetable stock

Takes 20 minutes • Serves 4

1 Cook the noodles in a pan of salted boiling water for 5 minutes, adding the broccoli for the last 2 minutes. Drain.
2 Meanwhile, heat a wok or frying pan until very hot. Add the oil, then stir in the ginger and garlic. Cook for 30 seconds, stirring. Add the chicken strips and cook for 5 minutes, stirring often, until tinged brown. Add the spring onions and stir briefly to heat through.
3 Mix the soy sauce and stock together and stir into the pan. Tip the drained noodles and broccoli into the pan, season with black pepper and toss everything together. Serve immediately.

• Per serving 417 kcalories, protein 30g, carbohydrate 49g, fat 12g, saturated fat 1g, fibre 3g, added sugar none, salt 2.61g

Stretch two chicken breasts to feed four in
this unusual salad with a tangy dressing.

Warm Thai Noodle Salad

2 large boneless skinless
chicken breasts
175g/6oz dried medium egg noodles
2 good handfuls of greens, such as
Chinese leaf, finely shredded
2 carrots, cut into thin strips
8 spring onions, finely sliced
1 red pepper, seeded and
finely sliced
handful of fresh coriander leaves

FOR THE DRESSING
1 red chilli, seeded and
finely chopped
2 garlic cloves, finely chopped
1 tbsp finely chopped fresh
root ginger
2 tbsp soy sauce
juice of 1 lime
2 tbsp olive oil

Takes 30 minutes • Serves 4

1 Preheat the grill to high. Put the chicken
on a baking sheet and grill for 10–12 minutes
without turning, until cooked through.
Meanwhile, cook the noodles according to
the packet instructions. Drain and rinse in
cold running water to stop them sticking
together.
2 Mix the vegetables in a bowl. Thinly slice
the chicken and add to the bowl, along with
the noodles and coriander leaves.
3 Mix the dressing ingredients together with
two tablespoons of water, pour over the
salad and toss well. Serve immediately.

• Per serving 336 kcalories, protein 24g, carbohydrate
40g, fat 10g, saturated fat 1g, fibre 2g, added sugar
none, salt 1.7g

This tasty rub is also good on pork and lamb.
Try the chicken barbecued too.

Salt and Pepper Fried Chicken

200g carton Greek yogurt
2 tbsp chopped fresh mint
juice of 1 lemon
good sprinkling of salt
(sea salt is best)
1 heaped tbsp coarsely crushed
peppercorns (buy them or crush
your own with a rolling pin)
4 boneless skinless chicken breasts
2 tbsp oil
new potatoes and salad, to serve

Takes 20 minutes • Serves 4

1 Mix together the yogurt and mint with a squeeze of lemon juice; season and set aside. Mix together the salt and peppercorns. Drizzle the chicken breasts with a little lemon juice, then rub the salt and pepper mixture evenly over each breast.

2 Heat the oil in a large frying pan. Add the chicken and cook for 6–7 minutes on each side until the chicken is cooked through and golden.

3 Squeeze over the remaining lemon juice. Serve the chicken with the minty yogurt, new potatoes and a salad.

• Per serving 262 kcalories, protein 37g, carbohydrate 2g, fat 12g, saturated fat 4g, fibre none, added sugar none, salt 0.56g

This spicy rub makes the skin deliciously crisp.
Cajun seasoning is available in most supermarkets.

Cajun-spiced Chicken

2 tbsp plain flour
2 tsp Cajun seasoning
½ tsp salt
4 boneless chicken breasts,
about 140g/5oz each in weight
2 tbsp olive oil
tzatziki (yogurt and cucumber
salad), mixed salad and new
potatoes, to serve

Takes 20 minutes • Serves 4

1 Mix together the flour, Cajun seasoning and salt.
2 Rub both sides of the chicken breasts with a tablespoon of the olive oil. Dust each side with the seasoned flour. Heat the remaining oil in a frying pan.
3 Fry the coated chicken for 6–7 minutes on each side until cooked and the skin is golden and crispy. Serve with the tzatziki, salad and new potatoes.

• Per serving 238 kcalories, protein 35g, carbohydrate 8g, fat 8g, saturated fat 1g, fibre none, added sugar none, salt 0.84g

This sticky glaze turns bland
chicken breasts into something really special.

Glazed Lemon Pepper Chicken

4 skinless boneless chicken breasts
4 tbsp clear honey
finely grated zest and juice 1 lemon
2 garlic cloves, crushed
1 tbsp Dijon mustard
2 tsp freshly ground black pepper
750g/1lb 10oz baby salad
potatoes or larger ones, halved
steamed broccoli florets, to serve

Takes 15 minutes, plus marinating •
Serves 4

1 Slash each chicken breast two or three times with a sharp knife. In a shallow dish mix the honey, lemon zest and juice, garlic, mustard and black pepper.

2 Add the chicken and turn to coat. Leave to marinate for 30 minutes or preferably overnight.

3 Preheat the oven to 220°C/Gas 7/fan oven 200°C. Arrange the potatoes and chicken in a single layer in a shallow-sided roasting tin and pour any excess marinade on top. Roast for 25–30 minutes or until the potatoes are tender and the chicken is cooked. Serve with broccoli and any pan juices.

• Per serving 339 kcalories, protein 38g, carbohydrate 44g, fat 3g, saturated fat 1g, fibre 2g, added sugar 11g, salt 0.55g

Removing the skin from chicken breasts reduces
the fat content. Coat them with a tasty glaze instead.

Maple and Orange-glazed Chicken

4 boneless skinless chicken breasts
3 tbsp maple syrup
1 tbsp wholegrain mustard
grated zest of 1 orange
1 tbsp soy sauce
dressed salad leaves, to serve

Takes 25 minutes • Serves 4
(easily doubled)

1 Make several diagonal slashes across each chicken breast. Tip the other ingredients into a wide shallow bowl and mix them together.

2 Add the chicken breasts and turn them in the mixture until evenly coated. At this point you can cover the dish with cling film and chill the chicken for 24 hours, if you don't want to cook them straightaway.

3 Preheat the grill or light the barbecue. Cook the chicken for 5–6 minutes each side, turning once and brushing or spooning over more marinade as you go, until the chicken is browned and glossy. Serve the chicken on a bed of dressed salad leaves.

• Per serving 216 kcalories, protein 26g, carbohydrate 8g, fat 9g, saturated fat 2g, fibre none, added sugar 11g, salt 1g

This simple recipe uses only six ingredients.
It also works well with pork steaks.

Chicken with Apples and Cider

2 tbsp oil
4 boneless skinless chicken breasts
1 onion, cut into wedges
2 eating apples, such as Cox's,
peeled, cored and each
cut into 8 wedges
300ml/½ pint dry cider
150ml/¼ pint chicken stock
rice or mashed potato, to serve

Takes 35 minutes • Serves 4

1 Heat the oil in a large frying pan and fry the chicken breasts for 3–4 minutes on each side until golden. Remove from the pan and set aside. Lower the heat slightly and add the onion. Fry, stirring, for 2–3 minutes until tinged brown. Add the apple and cook over a high heat for 5 minutes until golden.

2 Still over a high heat, pour in the cider and bubble for 2 minutes to reduce slightly. Add the stock, stirring to scrape the bits from the bottom of the pan. Lower the heat.

3 Return the chicken to the pan, cover and simmer for 5 minutes until it is almost cooked. Remove lid and simmer for 3–4 minutes to thicken the sauce a little. Season and serve with rice or mashed potato.

• Per serving 269 kcalories, protein 34g, carbohydrate 12g, fat 7g, saturated fat 1g, fibre 2g, added sugar none, salt 0.36g

A sweet cider blends well with the mustard tang.
Serve straight from the pan for supper.

Cider and Mustard Chicken

2 tbsp vegetable oil
2 onions, sliced
8 skinless boneless chicken thighs
2 garlic cloves, finely chopped
1 tbsp plain flour
300ml/½ pint sweet cider
1 tbsp wholegrain mustard
boiled potatoes and cabbage,
to serve

Takes 40 minutes • Serves 4

1 Heat the oil in a large pan, then fry the onions for 8–10 minutes, stirring often, until browned. Push them to one side of the pan, add the chicken thighs to the pan (with an extra splash of oil if necessary).
2 Sprinkle with the garlic and cook over a high heat for about 10 minutes, turning the chicken thighs until browned all over.
3 Sprinkle the flour over the chicken and cook for 1 minute, stirring. Stir in the cider and bubble over a medium to high heat for 2 minutes, stirring occasionally to thicken and reduce the sauce slightly. Stir in the mustard, then simmer, covered, for 10 minutes. Season and serve with potatoes and cabbage.

• Per serving 260 kcalories, protein 27g, carbohydrate 12g, fat 10g, saturated fat 2g, fibre 1g, added sugar none, salt 0.5g

This recipe is based on a tikka marinade but instead of curry powder, it uses red Thai curry paste and chopped coriander.

Thai-spiced Chicken

8 skinless chicken thighs
350g/12oz natural low fat yogurt
2–3 tbsp Thai red curry paste
4 tbsp chopped fresh coriander
7.5cm/3in piece cucumber
lime wedges and salad leaves,
to serve

Takes 55 minutes, plus marinating •
Serves 4 (easily doubled)

1 Preheat the oven to 200°C/Gas 6/fan oven 180°C. Put the chicken in a shallow dish in one layer. Blend a third of the yogurt, the curry paste and three tablespoons of the coriander. Season well with salt and pour over the chicken, turning the pieces until they are evenly coated. Leave for at least 10 minutes, or in the fridge overnight.
2 Lift the chicken on to a rack in a roasting tin and roast for 35–40 minutes, until golden. (To cook the chicken on the barbecue, reduce the cooking time to 25–30 minutes.)
3 Blend together the remaining yogurt and coriander. Finely chop the cucumber and stir into the yogurt mixture. Season. Serve with the chicken and garnish with wedges of lime and salad leaves.

• Per serving 266 kcalories, protein 43g, carbohydrate 8g, fat 7g, saturated fat 2g, fibre trace, added sugar none, salt 0.69g

Serve these mildly flavoured tasty skewers with Thai
fragrant rice and pak choi stir-fried in a little oil.

Chicken Skewers with Cucumber Dip

500g/1lb 2oz boneless skinless
chicken breasts
4 tbsp chopped coriander
1 tsp coarsely ground black pepper
juice of 2 limes
1 tsp light muscovado sugar
2 garlic cloves, crushed
1 tbsp vegetable oil
rice and pak choi, to serve

FOR THE DIP
125ml/4fl oz rice vinegar
2 tbsp sugar
1 red chilli, seeded and
finely chopped
1 shallot, thinly sliced
1 cucumber

Takes 30 minutes • Serves 4

1 Cut the chicken into thin slices. Mix the
coriander, pepper, lime juice, sugar, garlic
and oil. Toss the chicken in this mixture, then
thread on to 12 bamboo skewers. (You can
make these up to a day ahead and chill until
ready to cook.)
2 Make the dip. Heat the vinegar and sugar
in a small pan until the sugar has dissolved,
then increase the heat and boil for 3 minutes,
until slightly syrupy. Remove from the heat
and stir in the chilli and shallot. Leave to cool.
3 Quarter a 5cm/2in piece of cucumber,
then thinly slice and add to the dip. Cut the
rest of the cucumber into thin sticks.
4 Cook the chicken under a preheated grill
for 3–4 minutes each side, then serve with
the dipping sauce, cucumber sticks, rice
and pak choi.

• Per serving 210 kcalories, protein 31g, carbohydrate
12g, fat 4g, saturated fat 1g, fibre 1g, added sugar
9g, salt 0.22g

There is no need to add flour to thicken the sauce as the
tomatoes break down slightly, thickening the juices.

Chicken with Tomatoes and Coriander

25g/1oz butter
4 boneless skinless chicken breasts,
cut into bite-size pieces
450g/1lb baby new potatoes
2 tsp ground coriander
2 tsp ground cumin
300ml/½ pint hot chicken stock
750g/1lb 10oz ripe tomatoes,
cut into quarters
splash of Tabasco
squeeze of lemon juice
handful of chopped fresh coriander

Takes 40 minutes • Serves 4

1 Melt the butter in a large, deep-sided
frying pan. Add the chicken pieces and
potatoes and stir over a medium heat for
5–7 minutes until the chicken browns.
Add the spices and cook for 1 minute.
2 Pour in the stock and cook, covered, for
10 minutes until the potatoes are just tender.
Remove the lid for the last 3 minutes of
cooking. Add the tomatoes and cook over
a medium heat, stirring occasionally, for
5 minutes until the tomatoes are hot and
slightly softened.
3 Season and add a good splash of
Tabasco. Squeeze over a little lemon juice
and sprinkle with coriander. Serve hot.

• Per serving 325 kcalories, protein 38g, carbohydrate
26g, fat 8g, saturated fat 4g, fibre 3g, added sugar
none, salt 0.71g

A colourful sweet and sour stir fry,
great with rice or noodles.

Chinese Chicken with Pineapple

1 tbsp vegetable oil
1 garlic clove, finely chopped
4 boneless skinless chicken breasts,
cut into bite-size pieces
227g can pineapple chunks
in natural juice
2 carrots, cut into thin sticks
1 tbsp cornflour
juice of 1 lemon
2 tbsp tomato purée
3 tbsp light soy sauce
bunch of spring onions, trimmed
and halved lengthways
rice or noodles, to serve

Takes 25 minutes • Serves 4

1 Heat the oil in a wok or frying pan.
Add the garlic, stir briefly, then add the
chicken. Cook, stirring, for 10 minutes.
2 Drain the pineapple chunks (save the
juice). Add them to the pan with the carrots.
Cook, stirring, for 2–3 minutes.
3 Add water to the reserved pineapple
juice to make 200ml/7fl oz. Mix the cornflour
with the lemon juice, then stir in the purée,
soy sauce and diluted pineapple juice. Pour
over the chicken and add the spring onions.
Cook for 2 minutes more, stirring. Serve
immediately with rice or noodles.

• Per serving 525 kcalories, protein 42g, carbohydrate
82g, fat 5g, saturated fat 1g, fibre 2g, added sugar
none, salt 1.99g

Adding a good splash of soy as the chicken cooks
helps it go an even brown colour, and boosts the flavour.

Chicken and Broccoli Stir Fry

25g/1oz butter
450g/1lb boneless skinless chicken
breasts, cut into thin strips
3 tbsp dark soy sauce
350g/12oz broccoli,
broken into small florets
225g/8oz green beans, halved
1 bunch spring onions,
cut into long slices
2 tsp cornflour
juice of 2 oranges
25g/1oz fresh basil, roughly torn
rice or noodles, to serve

Takes 30 minutes • Serves 4
(easily halved)

1 Heat the butter in a wok or large frying pan. Add the chicken strips and a splash of soy sauce and cook for 5 minutes, stirring, until the chicken starts to brown.
2 Stir in the broccoli, beans and half the spring onions and cook for 3 minutes until just cooked.
3 Mix the cornflour with the orange juice and remaining soy sauce. Pour into the pan and cook for about 1 minute, stirring, until just thickened. Scatter in the basil and remaining spring onions. Serve with rice or noodles.

• Per serving 273 kcalories, protein 40g, carbohydrate 11g, fat 8g, saturated fat 4g, fibre 4g, added sugar none, salt 2.4g

There's very little shopping required
for this simple recipe.

Spicy Chicken and Apricot Stew

2 tbsp oil
8 boneless skinless chicken thighs,
cut into chunks
1 large onion, sliced
2 tsp plain flour
2 tsp ground cumin
2 tsp ground coriander
1 tsp paprika
600ml/1 pint chicken stock
12 ready-to-eat dried apricots
rice and peas, to serve

Takes 1 hour • Serves 4

1 Heat half the oil in a large pan, add the chicken and fry for 7 minutes until golden. Remove and set aside. Add the remaining oil and the onion and cook for 5 minutes until browned. Return the chicken to the pan.
2 Sprinkle in the flour and spices and cook, stirring, for 1–2 minutes. Slowly pour in the stock, stirring, so it sizzles and the sauce turns a rich colour. Simmer for 15 minutes.
3 Stir in the apricots and simmer for a further 15 minutes. Taste and season. Serve with rice and peas.

• Per serving 349 kcalories, protein 41g, carbohydrate 20g, fat 12g, saturated fat 3g, fibre 3g, added sugar none, salt 1.59g

Mi-cuit plums are half cooked and so they are
the softest juiciest plums to use in this recipe.

Spiced Plum Chicken

2 tsp olive oil
1 onion, chopped
1 garlic clove, finely chopped
1 tsp turmeric
½ tsp each ground cinnamon,
coriander and ginger
3 boneless skinless chicken breasts,
sliced into strips
284ml carton chicken stock
2 tbsp tomato purée
200g box mi-cuit plums, or ready-
to-eat prunes, stoned and halved
250g/9oz couscous
handful of chopped fresh coriander,
to serve

Takes 45 minutes • Serves 4

1 Heat the oil in a deep-sided frying pan.
Add the onion and cook for 5 minutes until
just golden. Add the garlic and cook for a
minute only, then add the spices and stir for
a minute. Add the chicken strips and cook
for 4–5 minutes until browned.
2 Add the stock and purée, and season.
Cook for 15–20 minutes, adding the plums
for the last 5 minutes.
3 Meanwhile, cook the couscous according
to the packet instructions; keep warm. Divide
the chicken and plums between plates,
sprinkle with coriander and serve with the
couscous.

• Per serving 360 kcalories, protein 32g, carbohydrate
52g, fat 4g, saturated fat 1g, fibre 3g, added sugar
15g, salt 0.5g

Turkey is one of the cheapest meats to buy and is really low in fat, with just 1.75g fat per 100g skinless cooked meat.

Cajun Turkey Steaks

450g/1lb small new potatoes
225g/8oz runner beans, trimmed
and thickly sliced
2 tbsp Cajun seasoning
4 turkey steak fillets
3 tbsp olive oil
finely grated zest and juice 1 lemon
1 garlic clove, crushed
3 firm tomatoes, seeded and cut
into chunks

Takes 30 minutes • Serves 4

1 Boil the potatoes for 8 minutes. Add the runner beans, cover and cook for a further 4 minutes.
2 Meanwhile, sprinkle the Cajun seasoning on to both sides of each turkey steak. Heat one tablespoon of oil in a large shallow frying pan and fry the turkey steaks for 3–4 minutes on each side until they start to blacken. Add the lemon zest and juice, and bubble briefly to reduce slightly.
3 Drain the potatoes and beans. Warm the remaining oil in the pan; stir in the vegetables, garlic and tomatoes. Cook for 1–2 minutes, tossing until the vegetables are just coated. Serve with the turkey and pan juices.

• Per serving 326 kcalories, protein 34g, carbohydrate 23g, fat 12g, saturated fat 2g, fibre 3g, added sugar none, salt 0.21g

This hot turkey salad is easily doubled for a crowd.
Try it in sandwiches too.

Barbecue Turkey Strips

2 tbsp dark muscovado sugar
4 tbsp clear honey
4 tbsp soy sauce
450g/1lb turkey strips
2 tbsp each olive oil and lemon juice
2 tsp caster sugar
1 cos lettuce, torn into pieces
2 large carrots, cut into sticks
100g/4oz fresh beansprouts

Takes 35 minutes, plus marinating •
Serves 4

1 Mix the muscovado sugar, half the honey
and half the soy sauce in a shallow dish.
Add the turkey strips and stir to coat.
Cover and leave to marinate for 30 minutes.
2 Thread the turkey on to eight skewers
(soak wooden ones for 20 minutes before
using to prevent them burning) and cook
under a preheated grill or barbecue for
6 minutes each side.
3 Whisk the remaining honey and soy
sauce with the olive oil, lemon juice and
caster sugar. Season and toss with the
lettuce and vegetables. Pile on to four
plates and put the turkey on top. Serve
immediately.

• Per serving 318 kcalories, protein 29g, carbohydrate
37g, fat 7g, saturated fat 1g, fibre 2g, added sugar
29g, salt 2.91g

Keep the heat high while cooking the turkey so it sizzles
to a good brown colour – this dramatically enhances flavour.

Sweet and Sour Turkey

1 tbsp vegetable oil
300g/10oz turkey strips, cut into
smaller strips if necessary
2 × 200g pack mixed baby carrots,
sweetcorn and mangetout
1 red pepper, seeded and sliced
225g/8oz beansprouts
finely grated zest and juice
of 1 small orange
3 tbsp soy sauce
1 tsp clear honey
2 tsp cornflour
2 garlic cloves, finely chopped
cooked rice or noodles, to serve

Takes 20–25 minutes • Serves 4

1 Heat the oil in a wok or frying pan and
fry the turkey for 3 minutes, stirring, until
browned.
2 Add the baby vegetables and pepper and
fry for 4 minutes. Stir in the beansprouts.
3 Mix the orange zest and juice, soy sauce,
honey, cornflour and garlic together. Pour
over the stir fry and let it bubble, stirring.
When the sauce has thickened, serve with
rice or noodles.

• Per serving 411 kcalories, protein 24g, carbohydrate
68g, fat 7g, saturated fat 1g, fibre 4g, added sugar
3g, salt 1.87g

Turkey mince is ideal for low-fat burgers.
Don't overcook them or they will be dry.

Spicy Turkey Burgers

450g/1lb turkey mince
1 tbsp dark soy sauce
1–2 tbsp sweet chilli sauce
zest and juice of 1 lemon
2 spring onions, finely chopped
tzatziki (yogurt and cucumber
salad), green salad and new
potatoes, to serve

Takes 35 minutes • Serves 4

1 Mix the turkey mince, dark soy sauce, sweet chilli sauce, lemon zest and juice, spring onions and plenty of salt and freshly ground black pepper until they are well combined.

2 Divide the mixture into four equal portions and shape into burgers.

3 Cook under a preheated hot grill for 8 minutes on each side until cooked through. If you want to barbecue them, cook away from the direct heat of the coals for 6–8 minutes, turning frequently until just beginning to char. Serve with the tzatziki, mixed green salad leaves and new potatoes.

• Per serving 125 kcalories; protein 26g, carbohydrate 1g, fat 2g, saturated fat 1g, fibre none, added sugar 1g, salt 1.13g

Substitute turkey mince for lamb or beef
to make a low-fat pasta sauce.

Turkey Bolognese

2 tbsp vegetable oil
1 large onion, chopped
2 garlic cloves, finely chopped
500g/1lb 2oz turkey mince
400g can chopped tomatoes
2 tbsp tomato purée
300ml/½ pint chicken or beef stock
350g/12oz spaghetti
1 large courgette, finely chopped
6 tomatoes, seeded and chopped
small handful of chopped parsley,
to serve

Takes 40 minutes • Serves 4

1 Heat the oil in a large saucepan and fry the onion and garlic for 4–5 minutes over a low heat until softened. Stir in the turkey mince and cook for 5 minutes, stirring frequently. Stir in the chopped tomatoes, tomato purée and stock. Bring to the boil then simmer, uncovered, for 10 minutes.
2 Meanwhile, cook the spaghetti according to the packet instructions. Stir the courgette and fresh tomatoes into the sauce and simmer for 5–6 minutes. Season.
3 Drain the pasta and divide between four plates. Spoon the sauce over and serve, scattered with parsley.

• Per serving 546 kcalories, protein 43g, carbohydrate 76g, fat 10g, saturated fat 2g, fibre 6g, added sugar none, salt 0.75g

Skirt steak is mainly used for braising but cooked
this way you'll get succulent meat at a low price.

Barbecued Balsamic Beef

600g/1lb 5oz thick piece
beef skirt or rump steak
2 shallots, very finely chopped
2 tbsp balsamic vinegar,
plus a little extra
500g/1lb 2oz new potatoes
250g bag washed spinach
2 tbsp olive oil, plus a litte extra

Takes 30 minutes, plus marinating •
Serves 4

1 Put the beef in a wide shallow dish and
rub it all over with the shallots and balsamic
vinegar. Season and leave to marinate for
20 minutes.
2 Slice the potatoes and cook in salted
boiling water for 12–15 minutes, until just
tender. Add the spinach and cover the pan
for a couple of minutes to wilt it. Drain well,
toss in two tablespoons of olive oil, and
season. Keep warm.
3 Meanwhile, grill or barbecue the beef
for 6–8 minutes on each side for skirt or
3–4 minutes each side for rump, depending
on thickness. Remove and cover with foil
for 5 minutes. Uncover and slice thinly
across the grain. Serve piled on top of the
potatoes and spinach, sprinkled with a little
extra vinegar and olive oil.

• Per serving 324 kcalories, protein 37g, carbohydrate
23g, fat 10g, saturated fat 3g, fibre 2.6g, added sugar
none, salt 0.49g

*This recipe works really well with
lean pork escalopes too.*

Steak with Mustard Vegetables

450g/1lb new potatoes,
halved lengthways
350g/12oz broccoli florets
finely grated zest and
juice of 2 oranges
2 garlic cloves, crushed
1 tbsp wholegrain mustard
2 tbsp clear honey
2 small orange peppers, cored,
seeded and cut into chunks
1 tsp vegetable oil
4 lean thin frying steaks

Takes 25 minutes • Serves 4

1 Cook the potatoes in lightly salted boiling
water for 5–6 minutes. Add the broccoli,
return to the boil, cook for 2–3 minutes
or until tender. Drain well and set aside to
keep warm.
2 Add the orange zest and juice to the pan,
with the garlic, mustard and honey. Bring to
the boil. Add the peppers. Cook on a high
heat until the juices start to thicken, about
1–2 minutes. Add the vegetables and keep
warm.
3 Heat a griddle pan. Brush the steaks
with the oil and season on both sides. Put in
the pan and press with a fish slice. Cook for
2 minutes, turn over and cook for a further
1–2 minutes. Serve with the vegetables and
their pan juices.

• Per serving 317 kcalories, protein 34g, carbohydrate
31g, fat 7g, saturated fat 2g, fibre 5g, added sugar
6g, salt 0.4g

This rich fruity casserole is perfect served with
fluffy celeriac and potato mash.

Beef with Apricots

400g/14oz extra lean stewing beef,
cut into cubes
2 large onions, chopped
4 garlic cloves, crushed
100g/4oz dried apricots, halved
50g/2oz sun-dried tomato halves
(not in oil), roughly chopped
400g can chopped tomatoes

FOR THE MASH
450g/1lb floury potatoes, peeled
and cut into small chunks
1 small celeriac, about 650g/
1lb 7oz, peeled and cut
into small chunks
100ml/3½fl oz skimmed milk
a grating of nutmeg

Takes 1½ hours • Serves 4

1 In a non-stick pan, dry-fry the beef in two
batches on a high heat until browned.
Season, then set aside.
2 Fry the onions and garlic on a low heat
for 4 minutes (add water if they stick).
Return the beef to the pan. Add the apricots,
sun-dried tomatoes, tomatoes and 600ml/
1 pint water, bring to the boil, and simmer
for 1 hour, stirring occasionally.
3 About 25 minutes before the end of
cooking, boil the potatoes and celeriac.
Drain, add the milk, and mash until smooth.
Add the nutmeg, season to taste and serve
with the beef.

• Per serving 360 kcalories, protein 31g, carbohydrate
47g, fat 7g, saturated fat 2g, fibre 12g, added sugar
none, salt 0.98g

An easy one-pot meal.

Be sure to choose lean lamb, trimmed of fat.

Springtime Lamb Stew

1 tbsp olive oil
12 shallots, peeled
350g/12oz trimmed diced lamb from
the chump or loin fillet
350g/12oz new potatoes, scrubbed
and cut into chunks
12 baby carrots,
trimmed and peeled
150ml/¼ pint white wine
250ml/9fl oz vegetable stock
3 bay leaves
200g can chopped tomatoes
100g/4oz frozen peas
1 tbsp fresh chopped parsley
crusty bread, to serve

Takes 1 hour 10 minutes • Serves 4

1 Heat the oil in a large saucepan and add the shallots and lamb. Fry over a medium heat until they are starting to brown, about 8–10 minutes.

2 Add the potatoes, carrots, white wine, stock, bay leaves and tomatoes to the pan. Season and bring to the boil. Cover the pan and leave the stew to simmer gently over a medium heat for 25–30 minutes until the vegetables and lamb are tender.

3 Stir in the peas and cook for another 2–3 minutes until cooked. Scatter in the parsley, adjust the seasoning and serve with crusty bread.

• Per serving 291 kcalories, protein 23g, carbohydrate 21g, fat 11g, saturated fat 4g, fibre 6g, added sugar none, salt 0.58g

A mildly spicy chilli with red lentils
replacing the more usual kidney beans.

Lamb and Lentil Chilli

1 large onion, finely chopped
2 garlic cloves, crushed
200g can chopped tomatoes
1 small aubergine, about 300g/10oz,
cut into 1cm/½in dice
140g/5oz red split lentils
300g/10oz lean diced lamb
1 tsp turmeric
2 tsp mild chilli powder
2 tsp ground cumin
1 tsp ground coriander
1 tsp light muscovado sugar
1 tbsp lemon juice
small bunch coriander or mint,
roughly chopped
250ml/9fl oz very low-fat yogurt
basmati rice, to serve

Takes 1¼ hours • Serves 4

1 Put the onion and garlic into a large saucepan with 100ml/3½fl oz water. Bring to the boil and cook for 5 minutes, until softened and nearly all the water has been absorbed.
2 Add the tomatoes, aubergine, lentils, lamb, turmeric, chilli powder, cumin, coriander, sugar, lemon juice and 450ml/16fl oz water. Bring to the boil, cover and simmer for 1 hour, until tender.
3 Season well and stir in most of the coriander or mint and half the yogurt. Immediately remove from the heat. Serve with basmati rice and the remaining yogurt spooned on top. Sprinkle with the remaining coriander or mint.

• Per serving 305 kcalories, protein 28g, carbohydrate 32g, fat 8g, saturated fat 4g, fibre 4g, added sugar none, salt 0.4g

This is a very adaptable recipe, impressive enough to cook if you have friends visiting and you are short of time.

Pork with Pine Kernels

500g/1lb 2oz pork fillet
plain flour, for coating
good handful flatleaf parsley
2tbsp olive oil
25g/1oz pine kernels
grated zest of ½ lemon and juice of a whole lemon
1 tbsp clear honey
pappardelle or tagliatelle and salad, to serve

Takes 25 minutes • Serves 4

1 Cut the pork into 2cm/¾in thick slices. Toss in seasoned flour to coat very lightly and shake off excess. Coarsely chop the parsley. Heat one tablespoon of olive oil in a large frying pan, add the pork in a single layer and fry for 3 minutes on each side, or until browned. Remove and keep warm.
2 Add another tablespoon of oil to the pan, add the pine kernels and fry until lightly browned, then stir in the lemon zest, juice and honey. Bubble briefly, stirring to make a sauce.
3 Return the pork to the pan and scatter with parsley. Cook for 3 minutes, turning the pork, until thoroughly reheated. Serve with pappardelle or tagliatelle and salad.

• Per serving 212 kcalories, protein 28g, carbohydrate 4g, fat 9g, saturated fat 2g, fibre none, added sugar 4g, salt 0.2g

Pork fillet is low in fat and it cooks quickly.
Here it's used in a mild curry.

Spicy Pork and Aubergine

1½ tbsp olive oil
2 onions, sliced
1 small aubergine (about 250g/9oz),
trimmed and diced
500g/1lb 2oz lean pork, fillet,
trimmed of any fat and sliced
2 sweet red peppers, seeded and
cut into chunky strips
2–3 tbsp mild curry powder
400g can plum tomatoes
cooked basmati rice, to serve

Takes 35 minutes • Serves 4

1 Heat the oil in a large non-stick frying pan
with a lid. Tip in the onions and aubergine
and fry for 8 minutes, stirring frequently, until
soft and golden brown.
2 Tip in the pork and fry for 5 minutes,
stirring occasionally, until it starts to brown.
Mix in the pepper strips and stir fry for about
3 minutes until soft.
3 Sprinkle in the curry powder. Stir fry for
a minute, then pour in the tomatoes and
150ml/¼pint water. Stir vigorously, cover the
pan and leave the curry to simmer for
5 minutes until the tomatoes break down
to form a thick sauce (you can add a drop
more water if the mixture gets too thick).
Season and serve with basmati rice.

• Per serving 293 kcalories, protein 31g, carbohydrate
16g, fat 11g, saturated fat 2g, fibre 6g, added sugar
none, salt 0.4g

In this easy recipe everything is
cooked together in one pan.

Pork Fillet with Roast Vegetables

4 medium parsnips,
quartered lengthways
1 butternut squash, (about 650g/
1lb 7oz) peeled, seeded
and cut into chunks
2 red onions, each cut
into 8 wedges
1 tbsp olive oil
grated zest of 1 lemon
2 tsp pork seasoning or dried
mixed Italian herbs
500g/1lb 2oz lean pork tenderloin,
in one or two pieces
1 medium cooking apple
400ml/14fl oz chicken stock

Takes 1½ hours • Serves 4

1 Preheat the oven to 200°C/Gas 6/fan
oven 180°C. Put the vegetables into a
roasting pan. Drizzle with the olive oil.
Season and toss together.
2 On a plate mix the lemon zest and pork
seasoning or herbs. Roll the pork in the mix
and place on the vegetables. Roast for
40–50 minutes.
3 Peel and core the apple. Cut into
chunks. Put in the roasting tin. Add the
stock and cook for a further 15–20 minutes.
Cut the pork into thick slices and serve with
the vegetables and pan juices spooned over.

• Per serving 397 kcalories, protein 34g, carbohydrate
45g, fat 10g, saturated fat 2g, fibre 12g, added sugar
none, salt 0.85g

A colourful combination of pork,
fruit and mellow spices.

Pork Skewers with Red Cabbage

FOR THE CABBAGE
450g/1lb red cabbage, shredded
150ml/¼ pint ginger wine,
wine or stock
2 tbsp unrefined soft dark
brown sugar
2 tbsp white wine vinegar
5cm/2in fresh root ginger,
finely chopped

FOR THE PORK
400g/14oz lean pork tenderloin,
cut into 24 pieces
2 dessert apples, cut into 8 wedges
2 tbsp clear honey
2 tbsp wholegrain mustard
6 tbsp half-fat crème fraîche
sliced boiled potatoes, to serve

Takes 1 hour 20 minutes • Serves 4

1 Put the cabbage in a large pan with the other cabbage ingredients. Toss over a high heat for 5 minutes. Simmer, covered, on a low heat for 1 hour, stirring occasionally.

2 Meanwhile, thread alternately 3 pieces of pork and 2 apple wedges on eight skewers. Season. Gently heat the honey and mustard in a small pan. About 15 minutes before the cabbage is cooked, heat the grill. Cover the grill pan with foil. Arrange the skewers on top. Brush with the mustard mix and grill for 5–6 minutes. Turn, brush again and grill for 5–6 minutes until cooked.

3 Add crème fraîche to the glaze; heat gently. Arrange the cabbage on plates, with skewers on top and pan juices spooned over. Drizzle with the glaze and serve with sliced potatoes.

• Per serving 352 kcalories, protein 25g, carbohydrate 33g, fat 10g, saturated fat 10g, fibre 4g, added sugar 16g, salt 0.59g

A low-fat version of an old favourite.
Be sure to choose the sausages carefully.

Toad-in-the-hole

1 red onion, cut into wedges,
layers separated
8 thick low-fat pork sausages
1 tsp olive oil

FOR THE BATTER
100g/4oz plain flour
1 medium egg
300ml/½ pint skimmed milk
2 tsp wholegrain mustard
1 tsp fresh thyme leaves
steamed carrots and cabbage,
to serve

Takes 1 hour 20 minutes • Serves 4

1 Preheat the oven to 200°C/Gas 6/fan oven 180°C. Tip the onions into a small shallow non-stick tin (about 23 × 30cm/ 9 × 12in). Arrange the sausages on top of the onions, then add the oil and roast for 20 minutes.

2 While they are roasting, make the batter. Sift the flour into a bowl, drop the egg in the centre and beat in the milk a little at a time until it makes a smooth batter. Stir in the mustard and thyme and season.

3 Pour the batter quickly into the tin and return to the oven for 40 minutes until the batter is risen and golden. Serve with steamed carrots and cabbage.

• Per serving 293 kcalories, protein 23g, carbohydrate 36g, fat 7g, saturated fat 2g, fibre 1g, added sugar none, salt 2.36g

This zingy way with gammon is surprisingly healthy. Lean steaks are served with nutritious bulghar wheat and green vegetables.

Sticky Glazed Gammon

85g/3oz bulghar wheat
85g/3oz fresh or frozen peas or
petits pois (225g/8oz in the pod)
1 large leek, thinly sliced
1 orange, halved
1 tbsp Worcestershire sauce
1 tbsp clear honey
1 tsp Dijon mustard
2 lean gammon steaks
1 tbsp mint sauce

Takes 30 minutes • Serves 2

1 Preheat the grill to high. Tip the bulghar and 450ml/16fl oz cold water into a large saucepan, bring to the boil and simmer for 8 minutes. Toss in the peas and leek and bubble for 3–5 minutes more, until soft.
2 While the bulghar bubbles, make the glaze. Squeeze the juice of one orange half into a pan, stir in the Worcestershire sauce, honey and mustard and simmer for 2 minutes until sticky. Season the steaks with pepper only, put them on the grill rack and grill for 5–6 minutes each side, brushing frequently with the glaze.
3 When the bulghar is cooked, drain, season well and fork in the mint sauce. Cut each steak in half and serve on the bulghar, with the remaining orange half cut into segments.

• Per serving 465 kcalories, protein 45g, carbohydrate 55g, fat 8g, saturated fat 2g, fibre 5g, added sugar 7g, salt 6.89g

A simple dish packed with healthy vegetables.
You could use leftover ham, but make sure it is lean.

Ham and Vegetable Casserole

2 tbsp olive oil
1 large onion, chopped
500g/1lb 2oz waxy
new potatoes, halved
1 red pepper, seeded and
cut into chunks
500g/1lb 2oz ripe
tomatoes, quartered
150ml/¼ pint vegetable or
chicken stock
1 tsp dried or 1 tbsp chopped
fresh thyme
3 courgettes, about 375g total
weight, thickly sliced
175g/6oz slice thick ham,
cut into strips
handful chopped fresh parsley

Takes 45 minutes • Serves 4

1 Heat the oil in a large saucepan. Add the onion and cook, stirring often, for 8 minutes or until golden. Tip in the potatoes, pepper, tomatoes, stock and thyme. Season well.
2 Cover and cook for 25 minutes, stirring from time to time until the potatoes are almost tender and the tomatoes have begun to break down to form a sauce.
3 Add the courgettes, and simmer for 5 minutes. Stir in the ham and parsley and heat through. Season and serve.

• Per serving 272 kcalories, protein 16g, carbohydrate 34g, fat 9g, saturated fat 2g, fibre 5g, added sugar none, salt 1.35g

If you don't have camembert, use crumbled stilton,
grated gruyère or even mature cheddar instead.

Ham, Leek and Camembert Grill

600ml/1 pint chicken or
vegetable stock
700g/1lb 9oz scrubbed unpeeled
potatoes, thickly sliced
450g/1lb leeks (about
2 medium), sliced
100g/4oz wafer-thin ham
125g packet camembert,
thinly sliced

Takes 25 minutes • Serves 4

1 In a large pan, heat the stock to boiling, then add the potatoes. Cook for 15 minutes until just tender, adding the leeks for the last 5 minutes of cooking time. Drain, reserving four tablespoons of the stock.

2 Preheat the grill. Layer up the sliced potatoes and leeks with the ham in a shallow heatproof dish and season between the layers.

3 Pour over the reserved stock. Lay the cheese on top, then grill for 5 minutes until the cheese has melted and is beginning to brown. Serve immediately.

• Per serving 280 kcalories, protein 17g, carbohydrate 34g, fat 9g, saturated fat 5g, fibre 5g, added sugar none, salt 1.81g

Choose quite thin fish fillets so they cook
quickly without the pesto burning.

Herby Cod Grills

4 tbsp natural low fat yogurt
2 tbsp sun-dried tomato pesto
2 tbsp chopped fresh parsley or dill
2 cod or haddock fillets, about
175g/6oz each, skinned
salad and crusty bread, to serve

Takes 15 minutes • Serves 2
(easily doubled)

1 Preheat the grill. Mix the yogurt, pesto and one tablespoon of the parsley or dill. Season and pour over the fish fillets in a shallow ovenproof or microwaveable dish, covering them completely.

2 Grill for 4–5 minutes without turning until the fish fillets are cooked through to the middle. Or cover the dish with cling film and microwave on High for 3 minutes.

3 Sprinkle the remaining parsley or dill over the dish and serve with salad and crusty bread.

• Per serving 247 kcalories, protein 36g, carbohydrate 3g, fat 10g, saturated fat 4g, fibre 3g, added sugar none, salt 0.53g

Cod cooks very quickly so time it carefully –
just a few minutes too much can make it tough and dry.

Spiced Cod with Crispy Onions

4 cod fillets, 140g/5oz
each in weight
200g tub Greek yogurt
1 tbsp tikka masala paste
2 tbsp chopped fresh root ginger
juice of ½ lemon
225g/8oz long grain rice
140g/5oz green beans, halved
1 tbsp vegetable oil
1 small onion, finely sliced

Takes 25 minutes, plus marinating •
Serves 4

1 Put the fish in a single layer in a shallow heatproof dish. Mix together the yogurt, curry paste, half the ginger, and lemon juice. Season. Pour over the fish, turning to coat. Set aside for 30 minutes.

2 Preheat the grill to high. Cook the rice in boiling water for 12–15 minutes, adding the beans for the last 4 minutes. Grill the fish in its marinade for 8–10 minutes, until the cod is cooked.

3 Meanwhile, heat the oil in a pan. Fry the onion and remaining ginger for 8 minutes over a medium heat until golden and crisp. Drain on kitchen paper. Drain the rice well. Serve the fish with the marinade, rice and green beans. Top with the fried onions.

• Per serving 408 kcalories, protein 34g, carbohydrate 49g, fat 10g, saturated fat 3g, fibre 1g, added sugar none, salt 0.46g

Shallow-fried fish needs a light dusting of flour to protect it from the fierce heat, and it makes a tasty, golden crust.

Cod with Lemon and Parsley

2 cod fillets, about 175g/6oz each
seasoned flour
1 lemon
25g/1oz butter
1 heaped tbsp chopped parsley
new potatoes and greens or runner beans, to serve

Takes 20 minutes • Serves 2

1 Coat the cod fillets with the flour, dusting off any excess. Squeeze the juice from the lemon.
2 Heat half the butter in a frying pan. When it is bubbling, add the fish and cook over a fairly high heat until the underside is done, about 4–5 minutes. Using a fish slice, turn the fillets carefully and brown the other side. When the fish is just cooked (the flesh will start to flake and become opaque), add the remaining butter to the pan. When it is bubbling, stir in the lemon juice and season.
3 Bubble the sauce up until it is slightly thickened, then stir in the parsley. Serve with new potatoes and greens or runner beans.

• Per serving 277 kcalories, protein 34g, carbohydrate 9g, fat 12g, saturated fat 7g, fibre 1g, added sugar none, salt 0.77g

Mixed pepper antipasto is available in jars in
most supermarkets and delicatessens.

Mediterranean Cod

750g/1lb 10oz floury potatoes
2 tbsp olive oil
4 cod fillets, 140g/5oz
each in weight
225g/8oz chestnut mushrooms
8 tbsp mixed pepper antipasto
2 tbsp freshly grated parmesan

Takes 1 hour • Serves 4

1 Preheat the oven to 200°C/Gas 6/fan oven 180°C. Cut the potatoes into wedges and put in a roasting tin. Drizzle over the olive oil and stir well. Season. Cook in the middle of the oven for 45–50 minutes, stirring halfway through, until the potatoes are golden, crisp and cooked through.

2 Meanwhile, put the cod fillets in an ovenproof dish in a single layer. Season well. Slice the mushrooms and scatter over the fish.

3 Spread the mixed pepper antipasto over the top of the mushrooms. Put the fish in the oven on the shelf above the potato wedges 10 minutes before the wedges have finished cooking. Sprinkle the fish with the grated parmesan and serve hot with the potato wedges.

• Per serving 359 kcalories, protein 34g, carbohydrate 34g, fat 11g, saturated fat 2g, fibre 4g, added sugar none, salt 0.43g

Use your microwave to speed up the
cooking of the baked pototoes.

Smoked Haddock Bake

2 large baking potatoes
225g bag fresh baby leaf spinach
4 × 175g/6oz skinless undyed
smoked haddock fillets
4 tbsp half-fat crème fraîche
50g/2oz extra mature
cheddar, grated

Takes 45 minutes • Serves 4

1 Pierce the potatoes all over with a sharp knife. Microwave on High for 16 minutes. Leave to stand for 3 minutes, then slice thickly.
2 Scatter the fresh spinach into the base of a large microwaveable dish and arrange the potatoes on top. Place the fish on the top. Drop on spoonfuls of crème fraîche and sprinkle with cheese.
3 Cover with cling film and pierce several times. Microwave on High for 8 minutes. Stand for 2 minutes. Remove the cling film. Grill under a preheated grill for 3 minutes.

• Per serving 334 kcalories, protein 41g, carbohydrate 23g, fat 9g, saturated fat 9g, fibre 3g, added sugar none, salt 3.86g

Cooked peas add extra colour and
flavour to these simple fishcakes.

Smoked Haddock Fishcakes

450g/1lb peeled potatoes,
cut into chunks
2 eggs
225g/8oz skinless smoked haddock
4 tbsp milk
25g/1oz butter
175g/6oz frozen peas, cooked
100g/4oz white breadcrumbs
2 tbsp vegetable oil
salad, to serve

Takes 50 minutes • Serves 2

1 Preheat the oven to 200°C/Gas 6/fan oven 180°C. Boil the potatoes and eggs in salted water for 10–12 minutes. Meanwhile put the fish, milk and butter in a pan, season, cover and simmer for 4–5 minutes. Strain and reserve the liquor. Flake the fish.
2 Drain the potatoes and eggs. Shell the eggs and mash them with the potatoes. Add the liquor, season and stir in the fish and peas. Shape into six cakes. Press into the breadcrumbs, coating evenly.
3 Pour the oil into a roasting tin. Heat for 5 minutes in the oven. Add the fishcakes, coat in the oil and cook for 25–30 minutes, turning halfway through. Serve with salad.

• Per serving 252 kcalories, protein 15g, carbohydrate 27g, fat 10g, saturated fat 3g, fibre 3g, added sugar none, salt 1.22g

Salmon takes on the strong flavours
of Chinese cooking very well.

Soy Salmon with Sesame Stir Fry

4 salmon fillets, about
100g/4oz each
3 tbsp soy sauce
2 tbsp clear honey
finely grated zest and
juice of 1 lemon
2 garlic cloves, thinly sliced
2.5cm/1in piece fresh root ginger,
finely grated
8 spring onions, finely shredded

FOR THE STIR FRY
1 tsp sesame oil
100g/4oz mangetout
2 medium carrots,
cut into matchsticks
100g/4oz baby corn, halved
2 courgettes, cut into matchsticks

Takes 30 minutes, plus marinating •
Serves 4

1 Put the salmon in a shallow dish. Heat the soy sauce, honey, lemon zest and juice, garlic and ginger in a small saucepan with one tablespoon of water for 4 minutes. Pour over the salmon and scatter with most of the spring onions. Leave to marinate in the fridge for at least 30 minutes.

2 Heat the grill or a griddle pan. Remove the salmon, reserving the marinade. Grill or griddle the salmon for 8 minutes, turning once, until tender and golden.

3 Meanwhile, heat a wok or large frying pan to really hot and add the sesame oil. Add the mangetout, carrots and corn, and stir fry for 2 minutes. Add the courgettes and stir fry for 2 minutes. Add the reserved marinade and cook for 2–3 minutes. Serve with the salmon and remaining spring onion.

• Per serving 280 kcalories, protein 23g, carbohydrate 18g, fat 12g, saturated fat 2.5g, fibre 3g, added sugar none, salt 2.6g

This is a really simple dish that's delicious
served with fried rice or noodles.

Lemon-fried Mackerel

2 lemons
4 × 300g/10oz small mackerel or
4 × 150g/5oz fish fillets
1 tbsp vegetable oil
3 tbsp soy sauce
1 sugar cube, or 1 tsp sugar
stir-fried rice or noodles, to serve

Takes 25 minutes • Serves 4

1 Thinly slice one of the lemons. Season the fish then place the lemon slices down the length of each. Tie in place with string.
2 Heat the oil in a large frying pan and cook the fish, lemon-side down, for 3–4 minutes until well browned. Turn and cook the other side for 3 minutes.
3 Add the soy sauce, four tablespoons of water and the sugar to the pan. Squeeze in the juice of the remaining lemon and simmer for 2–3 minutes until the fish is cooked through. Serve on a bed of rice or noodles, spooning over the pan juices.

• Per serving 163 kcalories, protein 28g, carbohydrate 4g, fat 4g, saturated fat 1g, fibre none, added sugar 1.5g, salt 2.27g

Cheap cans of tomatoes are often a false economy.
Better to go for a good quality can and keep the fresh flavour.

Prawns with Tomato and Feta

3 tbsp olive oil
2 onions, finely chopped
2 × 400g cans chopped tomatoes
in rich tomato sauce
pinch of sugar
350g/12oz large peeled prawns,
thawed if frozen
100g/4oz feta
3 tbsp chopped fresh parsley
rice or pasta, to serve

Takes 20 minutes • Serves 4

1 Heat three tablespoons of olive oil in a frying pan, add the onions and fry gently for about 7 minutes, until softened and light brown. Add the tomatoes and a pinch of sugar and simmer for 5 minutes.
2 Throw in the prawns, season and cook gently for 5 minutes until the prawns are thoroughly hot.
3 Serve spooned over rice or pasta. Crumble over the feta and sprinkle with chopped parsley.

• Per serving 186 kcalories, protein 22g, carbohydrate 11g, fat 6g, saturated fat 3g, fibre 3g, added sugar trace, salt 1.54g

With a bag of frozen seafood mixture in the
freezer you can make a speedy version of a classic dish.

Quick Seafood Paella

1 tbsp sunflower oil
1 onion, finely chopped
1 red pepper, seeded and sliced
2 garlic cloves, finely chopped
230g can chopped tomatoes
1 tsp turmeric
300g/10oz long grain rice
1.3 litres/2¼ pints vegetable stock
450g bag frozen mixed seafood
(prawns, mussels and
squid rings), thawed
175g/6oz green beans, halved
handful of chopped fresh parsley
1 lemon, cut into wedges

Takes 30 minutes • Serves 4

1 Heat the oil in a large frying pan and cook the onion and pepper for 5 minutes until softened but not brown. Stir in the garlic, tomatoes and turmeric and cook for 1 minute more, stirring occasionally.
2 Tip in the rice and cook for 1 minute, stirring to coat the grains. Pour in the stock, stir well and bring to the boil, then simmer uncovered for 8 minutes, stirring occasionally, until the rice is almost cooked and most of the stock has been absorbed.
3 Add the seafood and beans and cook for 3–4 minutes more. Stir in the parsley and season. Serve straight from the pan with lemon wedges.

• Per serving 463 kcalories, protein 32g, carbohydrate 75g, fat 6g, saturated fat 1g, fibre 3g, added sugar none, salt 1.91g

Potatoes and canned beans make this simple supper a filling meal.
Serve with a leafy green salad.

Vegetable and Bean Bake

1 tbsp sunflower oil
2 large onions, thinly sliced
2 garlic cloves, crushed
1 tsp paprika
2 tbsp tomato purée
410g can cannellini beans,
drained and rinsed
2 tbsp fresh chopped parsley
2 large baking potatoes,
peeled and sliced
1 large courgette, sliced diagonally
4 ripe tomatoes, sliced
150ml/¼ pint vegetable stock
25g/1oz grated parmesan

Takes 1½ hours • Serves 4

1 Preheat the oven to 220°C/Gas 7/fan oven 200°C. Heat the oil in a pan. Gently fry the onion and garlic for 10 minutes. Stir occasionally. Add the paprika and cook for 1 minute. Add the tomato purée, beans and parsley. Tip into a 3 litre/5¼ pint shallow ovenproof dish.

2 Parboil the potatoes in lightly salted boiling water for 5 minutes. Drain and spread over the beans. Top with the courgettes and tomatoes.

3 Pour over the stock. Bake for 35 minutes, until tender. Sprinkle with cheese and cook for 10 minutes until golden.

• Per serving 304 kcalories, protein 14g, carbohydrate 50g, fat 7g, saturated fat 2g, fibre 8g, added sugar none, salt 0.57g

A light and colourful warm salad, making use
of couscous instead of rice or pasta.

Chargrilled Peppers with Couscous

50g/2oz couscous
2 tbsp sultanas or raisins
1 red pepper and ½ yellow
or orange pepper,
seeded and quartered
½ lemon, cut into wedges
1 tsp olive oil
2 tbsp chopped fresh parsley
or coriander

Takes 10 minutes • Serves 1

1 Put the couscous and sultanas or raisins in a bowl, pour over 150ml/¼ pint boiling water and leave for 5 minutes until the water is absorbed. Preheat the grill to high.
2 Put the peppers, skin-side up, on the grill rack with the lemon wedges, brush with oil and grill for 5 minutes until the pepper skins are blackened (leave the skins on for a smoky flavour). Stir the herbs into the couscous and season.
3 Spoon the couscous on to a plate, top with the peppers and squeeze the juice from the grilled lemon over. Serve immediately.

• Per serving 326 kcalories, protein 7g, carbohydrate 63g, fat 7g, saturated fat 1g, fibre 5g, added sugar none, salt 0.05g

Choose the brown-skinned sweet potatoes
with the attractive orange flesh.

Sweet Potato and Cauliflower Curry

1 tbsp vegetable oil
1 onion, chopped
1 garlic clove, crushed
2 tbsp medium curry powder
4 tsp plain flour
350g/12oz orange-fleshed sweet
potatoes (brown-skinned),
cut into cubes
350g/12oz cauliflower florets
850ml/1½ pints vegetable stock
100g/4oz green beans, trimmed
1 tsp garam masala
naan bread and lime wedges,
to serve

Takes 35 minutes • Serves 4

1 Heat the oil in a large pan and fry the onion for 2–3 minutes, stirring occasionally, until softened. Stir in the garlic, curry powder and flour and cook for a further minute.
2 Add the sweet potatoes to the pan along with the cauliflower and stock. Bring to the boil and simmer for 10–15 minutes until the potatoes are almost tender.
3 Stir in the green beans and garam masala and cook for 3 minutes. Serve with warm naan bread and wedges of lime.

• Per serving 257 kcalories, protein 9g, carbohydrate 44g, fat 6g, saturated fat 1g, fibre 6g, added sugar none, salt 0.81g

Thai curries are often thinner and hotter than
Indian curries, with fantastic vivid flavours.

Thai Red Vegetable Curry

1 tbsp vegetable oil
1 large onion, diced
500g/1lb 2oz sweet
potatoes, cubed
300g/10oz squash or
marrow, cubed
250g/9oz flat green beans
2 tomatoes, diced
2 × 400g cans coconut milk
2 tsp Thai red curry paste
juice of 1 large lime
2 tbsp soy sauce
handful fresh basil or coriander
boiled rice, to serve

Takes 35 minutes • Serves 6

1 Heat the oil in a large pan and cook
the onion, sweet potato and squash for
5 minutes until beginning to soften. Cut
the beans into 5cm/2in lengths, then add
these and the tomatoes and cook for a
further 2–3 minutes until the tomatoes begin
to soften.
2 Add the coconut milk and curry paste
and bring to the boil. Cook the mixture for
10–12 minutes until the vegetables are
tender.
3 Add the lime juice, soy sauce and fresh
basil or coriander; check the seasoning.
Serve with boiled rice.

• Per serving 170 kcalories, protein 4g, carbohydrate
34g, fat 3g, saturated fat trace, fibre 5g, added sugar
trace, salt 1.44g

This is ideal as a starter but could also be served as an energy-rich snack, just as delicious served hot or cold.

Stuffed Peppers

3 small baking potatoes, peeled and cut into 5mm slices
½ × 425g can pimientos, drained
1 red chilli, seeded and finely chopped
25g/1oz pine nuts, toasted
2 garlic cloves, crushed
4 tbsp sun-dried tomato paste
100g/4oz brown breadcrumbs
2 large red and 2 large yellow peppers, seeded and halved
handful fresh basil leaves
2 tbsp rosemary-infused olive oil
crusty bread, to serve

Takes 1 hour • Serves 8 (as a starter)

1 Preheat the oven to 200°C/Gas 6/fan oven 180°C. Cook the potatoes in lightly salted boiling water for 8 minutes. Drain and set aside. Place the pimientos, chilli, pine nuts, garlic, sun-dried tomato paste and breadcrumbs in a food processor and process to form a coarse paste.

2 Place the pepper halves, skin-side down, in a large roasting tin. Sandwich the potato slices with the pimiento paste and basil leaves and arrange, on their sides, in the pepper halves. Drizzle over the rosemary-infused oil and season.

3 Bake for 30 minutes until the peppers are cooked and the potatoes are tender. Serve immediately with crusty bread.

• Per serving 173 kcalories, protein 4g, carbohydrate 24g, fat 7g, saturated fat 1g, fibre 3g, added sugar none, salt 0.32g

A filling meal using the bottle-shaped squash.
Or serve the sauce with jacket potatoes.

Squash with Tomatoes and Chickpeas

2 medium-sized butternut squashes, about 700g/1lb 9oz each, halved lengthways and seeded
1 tbsp olive oil
1 tbsp balsamic vinegar
1 onion, roughly chopped
4 garlic cloves, peeled and very thinly sliced
400g can plum tomatoes
410g can chickpeas, drained and rinsed
300ml/½ pint vegetable stock
2 tbsp tomato purée
1 tsp caster sugar
large handful of baby spinach leaves

Takes 1 hour 20 minutes • Serves 4

1 Preheat the oven to 200°C/Gas 6/fan oven 180°C. Arrange the squash cut-side up in a large non-stick roasting tin. Brush with the oil and season generously. Drizzle with the balsamic vinegar and roast for 45 minutes until just tender.

2 Meanwhile, put the onion, garlic, tomatoes, chickpeas, stock, tomato purée and caster sugar into a large saucepan. Bring to the boil, break up the tomatoes slightly and simmer for 25 minutes, stirring occasionally until thickened.

3 Season to taste. Stir in the spinach and cook until just wilted. Serve the butternut squash with the sauce spooned over.

• Per serving 239 kcalories, protein 10g, carbohydrate 41g, fat 5g, saturated fat none, fibre 8g, added sugar 2g, salt 0.78g

The grated raw beetroot in the salad mix softens
during heating and gives the rice pretty flecks of pink.

Beetroot and Lamb's Lettuce Risotto

25g/1oz butter
1 onion, chopped
300g/10oz risotto rice
150ml/¼ pint dry white wine
850ml/1½ pints vegetable stock
50g/2oz freshly grated parmesan
150g bag beetroot and lamb's
lettuce salad

Takes 30 minutes • Serves 4

1 Melt half the butter in a pan with a lid. Stir in the onion and cook for 5 minutes until softened but not brown. Add the rice and cook for 3 minutes, stirring to coat the grains. Pour in the wine and bubble away. Stir in the stock and return to the boil. Cover the pan and simmer, without stirring, for 12–15 minutes, until the rice is just tender.
2 Remove from the heat, stir in the parmesan and remaining butter and season. Tip in the salad and stir gently until the leaves are wilted; take care not to overstir or the rice will turn too pink.
3 Divide between warm serving plates and serve sprinkled with freshly ground black pepper.

• Per serving 398 kcalories, protein 13g, carbohydrate 62g, fat 10g, saturated fat 6g, fibre 2g, added sugar none, salt 1.23g

The Italians serve soft polenta to soak up delicious sauces.
Here it is used to complement Asian flavours.

Soft Polenta with Pak Choi and Soy

1.4 litres/2½ pints vegetable stock
250g/9oz quick-cook polenta
1 tbsp Thai seven-spice paste
1 tbsp chilli sauce
1 tbsp soy sauce
1 tsp crushed garlic
1 tsp crushed ginger
1 tbsp sesame oil
1 red chilli, seeded and thinly sliced
140g/5oz shiitake
mushrooms, halved
4 heads pak choi,
halved lengthways

Takes 25 minutes • Serves 4

1 Pour the stock into a large pan and bring to a rolling boil. Shower in the polenta, stirring constantly. Stir in the Thai paste and simmer gently for 4–5 minutes, stirring. Season.

2 Mix the chilli sauce, soy sauce, garlic, ginger and two tablespoons of water together. Heat the sesame oil in a wok and stir-fry the chilli and mushrooms for 1 minute. Add the pak choi and four tablespoons of water and stir fry until the water has evaporated. Pour over the soy sauce mix and bring to the boil.

3 Divide the polenta between shallow serving bowls and top with the vegetables and dressing. Serve immediately.

• Per serving 272 kcalories, protein 9g, carbohydrate 48g, fat 6g, saturated fat 1g, fibre 2g, added sugar none, salt 1.82g

You know when gnocchi is cooked as it rises to the surface. Vary the recipe by adding peas, beans – or anything that takes your fancy.

Gnocchi Gratin

1 red pepper, seeded and quartered
400g pack fresh potato gnocchi
125g pack very low-fat garlic and herb soft cheese
75ml/2½fl oz dry white wine
large pinch of freshly grated nutmeg
85g/3oz baby spinach leaves
8 large basil leaves, roughly torn
garlic bread, to serve

Takes 20 minutes • Serves 2

1 Preheat the grill to hot. Grill the pepper quarters, skin-side up, for 7–8 minutes until charred. Place in a plastic bag, seal and leave to stand for 5 minutes to loosen the skins.

2 Bring a large pan of water to the boil and cook the gnocchi according to the packet instructions, until they rise to the surface. Meanwhile, in a separate pan warm the soft cheese, wine and nutmeg until melted and hot. Season to taste.

3 Remove the skin from the peppers and cut the flesh into strips. Toss with the gnocchi, spinach and basil, then pour the melted cheese sauce over. Serve immediately with garlic bread.

• Per serving 470 kcalories, protein 19g, carbohydrate 81g, fat 7g, saturated fat 4g, fibre 6g, added sugar none, salt 0.97g

A veggie version of the traditional Spanish rice dish. Smoked paprika adds extra flavour, but ordinary paprika works too.

Vegetable Paella

2 tbsp olive oil
1 onion, finely chopped
1 garlic clove, crushed
1 red pepper, seeded and finely chopped
1 green pepper, seeded and finely chopped
100g/4oz chestnut mushrooms, sliced
225g/8oz long grain rice
850ml/1½ pints vegetable stock
½ tsp smoked or ordinary paprika
large pinch of saffron strands
85g/3oz frozen peas
2 tomatoes, seeded and finely diced
2 tbsp chopped flatleaf parsley
green salad, to serve

Takes 35 minutes • Serves 4

1 Heat the oil in a frying pan and fry the onion for 2–3 minutes, stirring occasionally, until softened. Add the garlic, red and green peppers and mushrooms and cook for a further 2–3 minutes, stirring occasionally.

2 Stir in the rice and fry for 1 minute. Stir in the stock, paprika and saffron. Bring to the boil and simmer for 10–12 minutes, stirring occasionally, until the rice is just tender (top up with more water if necessary). Stir in the peas and cook for a further 2–3 minutes. Season to taste.

3 Spoon the paella on to serving plates and sprinkle over the tomato and parsley. Serve immediately with a green salad.

• Per serving 324 kcalories, protein 7g, carbohydrate 58g, fat 9g, saturated fat 1g, fibre 4g, added sugar none, salt 0.06g

The dimpled apricots look charming left whole, but you can halve and stone them before poaching if you prefer.

Summery Provençal Apricots

1 x 75cl bottle dry fruity rosé wine
175g/6oz golden caster sugar
1 vanilla pod, split open lengthways
with a sharp knife, then cut in 4
(keep the seeds inside)
700g/1lb 9oz ripe fresh apricots
vanilla ice-cream, to serve

Takes 40 minutes • Serves 4

1 Pour the wine into a saucepan, tip in the sugar and then add the pieces of vanilla pod. Stir over a low heat until the sugar has dissolved.

2 Add the apricots. Cover and gently poach until just softened – about 15–20 minutes for whole fruit and 10–15 minutes for halves.

3 Lift the apricots out with a slotted spoon and put them in a bowl. Boil the liquid hard for 8–10 minutes to make a thin syrup. Pour over the apricots and leave to cool. Serve warm or cold, with a piece of vanilla pod to decorate and a scoop of vanilla ice-cream.

• Per serving 356 kcalories, protein 2g, carbohydrate 62g, fat none, saturated fat 3g, fibre 3g, added sugar 46g, salt 0.03g

Choose an orange-fleshed melon for its colour and sweet flavour.
If you have time chill the melon cubes first.

Melon with Hot Redcurrant Sauce

finely grated zest and juice
of 1 orange
2 tbsp redcurrant jelly
1 ripe orange-fleshed melon
low-fat natural yogurt, to serve

Takes 10 minutes • Serves 4

1 Put the orange zest and juice in a pan with the redcurrant jelly and a splash of water. Heat gently, stirring occasionally, until the jelly has melted to a smooth sauce.
2 Cut the melon into quarters, discarding the seeds and the skin. Cut the flesh into 2.5cm/1in cubes and put in a bowl.
3 Pour the hot redcurrant sauce over the melon, stir well and serve with spoonfuls of yogurt.

• Per serving 66 kcalories, protein 1g, carbohydrate 16g, fat trace, saturated fat none, fibre 2g, added sugar none, salt 0.04g

A refreshing palate-cleansing sorbet – great after Mexican food.
But watch out as it has a kick of its own!

Tequila Sunrise Sorbet

225g/8oz caster sugar
juice of 2 limes
juice of 2 lemons
juice of 5 oranges
100ml/3½ fl oz tequila,
plus extra to serve
1 medium egg white
(uncooked eggs should be
avoided by those who are very
young, elderly or pregnant)
4 tbsp grenadine
orange and lime wedges, to serve

Takes 10 minutes, plus freezing •
Serves 6

1 Put 100ml/3½fl oz water into a large pan with the sugar and fruit juices. Cook over a low heat for 3–4 minutes, stirring until the sugar has dissolved. Boil for 1 minute. Cool completely. Stir in the tequila and chill.

2 Whisk the egg white until stiff and fold into the fruit syrup. Pour half the mixture into a freezerproof container and seal. Stir the grenadine into the other half, mix well and pour into a freezerproof container. Seal. Freeze for 2 hours until slushy around the edges. Break up any ice crystals with a fork and refreeze for a further 2 hours until solid.

3 Remove the sorbets from the freezer 20 minutes before serving. Frost the serving dishes with egg white and sugar. Scoop both sorbets into each dish. Pour over a shot of tequila and decorate with citrus wedges.

• Per serving 211 kcalories, protein 1g, carbohydrate 39g, fat 0.01g, saturated fat none, fibre 0.11g, added sugar 35g, salt 0.03g

Check the melons are really ripe and
fragrant for the best flavour.

Melon and Ginger Sorbet

2 ripe Galia melons
(about 1.5kg/3lb 5oz),
halved and seeded
75g/3oz caster sugar
4 pieces stem ginger in syrup,
drained and chopped
1 medium egg white
(uncooked eggs should be
avoided by those who are very
young, elderly or pregnant)

Takes 15 minutes, plus freezing •
Serves 4

1 Scoop out the flesh from the melons and place in a food processor with the sugar. Blend until smooth, then stir in the ginger and transfer to a shallow freezerproof dish. Freeze for 2 hours until mushy.
2 Whisk the egg white until just stiff, but not dry. Remove the iced melon from the freezer and mash with a fork, then stir in the egg white.
3 Return to the freezer for a further 2 hours until frozen. Serve decorated with extra stem ginger, if liked.

• Per serving 173 kcalories, protein 3g, carbohydrate 42g, fat 0.4g, saturated fat 0.01g, fibre 2g, added sugar 21g, salt 0.33g

Leave the brûlée topping until up to an hour
before serving as it slowly softens on standing.

Strawberry Yogurt Brûlées

500g/1lb 2oz strawberries
juice of 1 orange
500g carton natural yogurt
100g/4oz caster sugar

Takes 30 minutes, plus chilling •
Serves 6

1 Slice the strawberries and divide between six serving dishes or glasses. Sprinkle over the orange juice, then spoon over the yogurt. Chill until ready to serve.
2 Tip the sugar into a small pan with two tablespoons of cold water. Heat gently, stirring to dissolve the sugar, then increase the heat and stop stirring. Boil the mixture carefully until it turns a light caramel colour, then remove from the heat and plunge the base of the pan into a sink filled with cold water to stop it cooking further.
3 When the bubbles have subsided, carefully pour a little over each dessert. Leave for 10 minutes before serving or chill for up to an hour.

• Per serving 202 kcalories, protein 7g, carbohydrate 43g, fat 1g, saturated fat 1g, fibre 1g, added sugar 26g, salt 0.26g

For a special occasion, substitute half the apple
juice with 150ml/¼ pint of red wine.

Poached Pears with Blackberries

4 medium pears
zest of 1 lemon (peel off
with a potato peeler)
1 tbsp lemon juice
250g/9oz blackberries
300ml/½ pint unsweetened
apple juice
50g/2oz golden caster sugar
8 tbsp 0% fat natural Greek yogurt

Takes 40 minutes • Serves 4

1 Peel the pears but don't remove their
stalks. Place them in a saucepan with the
lemon zest and juice, half the blackberries,
the apple juice and caster sugar. Heat until
simmering, then cover and cook gently for
20–25 minutes until the pears are tender,
turning them once.
2 Remove the pears from the liquid and
cool for a few minutes. Halve each, core
with a teaspoon or melon baller, and transfer
to four dishes.
3 Strain the liquid through a sieve, into a pan.
Add the remaining blackberries and warm
gently. Serve the pears and blackberries with
the yogurt.

• Per serving 180 kcalories, protein 5g, carbohydrate
41g, fat 0g, saturated fat 0g, fibre 5g, added sugar
13g, salt trace

The apricots can be cooked up to two days ahead and stored in the fridge. Try serving it for breakfast too.

Banana and Apricot Compôte

250g/9oz ready-to-eat dried apricots
200ml/7fl oz apple juice
2 bananas, sliced
4 passion fruit (or a punnet of raspberries)
2 tbsp toasted flaked almonds
yogurt or crème fraîche, and biscuits, to serve

Takes 30 minutes, plus cooling • Serves 4

1 Put the apricots, apple juice and 200ml/7fl oz water in a pan. Bring to the boil, cover and simmer for 20 minutes.
2 Remove from the heat and leave to cool – you can make ahead up to this stage.
3 Tip the cooled apricots into a bowl and stir in the banana. Mix in the flesh from the passion fruit. Sprinkle the almonds over the fruit and serve with yogurt or crème fraîche, and biscuits.

• Per serving 341 kcalories, protein 7g, carbohydrate 71g, fat 5g, saturated fat trace, fibre 8g, added sugar none, salt 0.13g

A simple dessert with just four ingredients.
Serve with natural yogurt.

Marzipan and Mincemeat Apples

2 medium Bramley apples
85g/3oz marzipan, chopped
8 tbsp mincemeat
finely grated zest and juice of
1 small lemon
natural yogurt, to serve

Takes 25 minutes • Serves 4

1 Cut the apples in half widthways. Remove and discard the cores, then stand the apples in a microwave-proof dish. Mix the marzipan with the mincemeat and lemon zest. Spoon into the centre of the apples and spoon over the lemon juice.

2 Cover the dish with cling film, pierce several times and microwave on High for 4½ minutes. If you don't have a turntable and the apples are not cooking evenly, turn the dish halfway through.

3 Remove the cling film and leave to stand for 5 minutes before serving with natural yogurt.

• Per serving 200 kcalories, protein 2g, carbohydrate 41g, fat 4g, saturated fat 1g, fibre 2g, added sugar 24g, salt trace

This is an easy, no-fuss cherry and lemon
version of the classic French recipe.

Cheat's Clafoutis

450g/1lb cherries, pitted
2 tbsp cherry, plum or apricot jam
finely grated zest and juice
of 1 lemon
50g/2oz plain flour
3 large eggs
450ml/16fl oz skimmed milk
½ tsp ground cinnamon
3 tbsp golden caster sugar
icing sugar, to dust

Takes 50 minutes • Serves 2–3

1 Preheat the oven to 190°C/gas 5/fan
oven 170°C. Lightly oil a shallow 1.3 litre/
2¼ pint baking dish. Gently heat the cherries
and jam in a large saucepan, stirring until the
jam melts over the cherries. Tip them into the
dish and sprinkle with the lemon zest and
juice.
2 Whizz the flour, eggs, milk, cinnamon and
sugar in a food processor for 30 seconds
until smooth. Pour over the cherries.
3 Put the dish on a baking tray and bake
for 25–30 minutes or until the custard is set
and the jam is beginning to bubble through.
Dust with icing sugar and serve hot.

• Per serving 532 kcalories, protein 23g, carbohydrate
92g, fat 11g, saturated fat 3g, fibre 2g, added sugar
38g, salt 0.66g

Date purée replaces fat in this
tempting recipe, hence the title.

Guilt-free Sticky Toffee Puds

175g/6oz pitted dried dates
150ml/¼ pint maple syrup
1 tbsp vanilla extract
2 large eggs, separated
85g/3oz self-raising flour
0% Greek yogurt and extra maple
syrup, to serve (optional)

Takes 1½ hours • Serves 4

1 Preheat the oven to 180°C/Gas 4/fan oven 160°C. Simmer the dates in 175ml/ 6fl oz water for 5 minutes. Tip into a food processor, add six tablespoons of maple syrup and the vanilla, and blend until smooth. Transfer to a bowl and mix in the egg yolks, followed by the flour.
2 Whisk the egg whites until stiff, and fold into the date mixture. Put one tablespoon of maple syrup into each of four 200ml/7fl oz pudding moulds. Add the mixture. Cover each tightly with foil, stand in an ovenproof dish and pour in hot water to halfway up the sides of the moulds. Cook for 1 hour, until a skewer inserted into the centre comes out clean.
3 Uncover, run a knife around the edges, and invert on to plates. Drizzle over yogurt and maple syrup to serve.

• Per serving 339 kcalories, protein 7g, carbohydrate 73g, fat 4g, saturated fat 1g, fibre 2g, added sugar 25g, salt 0.33g

Index

Picture credits and recipe credits

BBC Worldwide would like to thank the following for providing photographs. While every effort has been made to trace and acknowledge all photographers, we would like to apologise should there be any errors or omissions.

Chris Alack p53, p59, p111; Iain Bagwell p73, p141, p161, p203; Clive Bozzard-Hill p175; Jean Cazals p15, p37; Ken Field p45, p95, p123, p153, p199; Hulton Archive p55; David Jordan p181, p189; Dave King p117, p119, p125, p163; Richard Kolker p191; Steve Lee p79; David Munns p13, p21, p35, p39, p81, p107, p155, p159; Myles New p43, p89, p139, p211; Nick Pope p33; Bill Reavell p177; Simon Smith p185; Roger Stowell p17, p19, p23, p27, p31, p41, p47, p63, p65, p77, p83, p87, p91, p93, p99, p101, p105, p109, p115, p121, p131, p143, p149, p151, p171, p183, p193, p195, p201, p207; Martin Thompson p11, p57, p69; Martin Thompson and Philip Webb p113; Trevor Vaughan p187; Simon Walton p51, p61, p75, p85, p133, p135, p147, p165, p209; Philip Webb p157; Simon Wheeler p67, p71, p97, p103, p127, p137, p145, p169; Jonathan Whitaker p29, p129, p173; Frank Wieder p197; Geoff Wilkinson p167, p179, p205; BBC Worldwide p25, p49

All the recipes in this book have been created by the editorial teams on *BBC Good Food Magazine* and *BBC Vegetarian Good Food Magazine*.

Angela Boggiano, Lorna Brash, Sara Buenfeld, Mary Cadogan, Gilly Cubitt, Barney Desmazery, Joanna Farrow, Rebecca Ford, Silvana Franco, Catherine Hill, Jane Lawrie, Clare Lewis, Sara Lewis, Liz Martin, Kate Moseley, Orlando Murrin, Vicky Musselman, Angela Nilsen, Justine Pattison, Jenny White and Jeni Wright.